James Capper

Observations on the Passage to India Through Egypt.

Edn. 3

James Capper

Observations on the Passage to India Through Egypt.
Edn. 3

ISBN/EAN: 9783337809478

Printed in Europe, USA, Canada, Australia, Japan

Cover: Foto ©ninafisch / pixelio.de

More available books at **www.hansebooks.com**

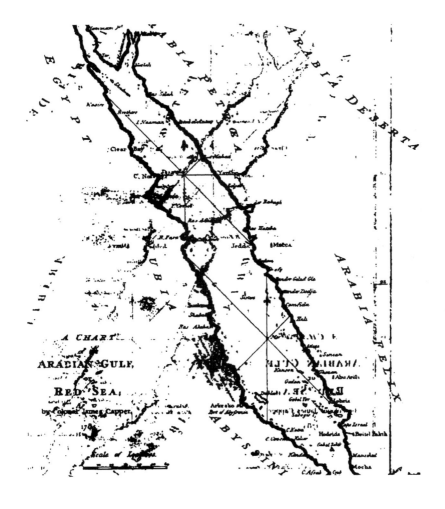

OBSERVATIONS

ON THE

PASSAGE TO INDIA,

THROUGH EGYPT.

ALSO

By VIENNA through CONSTANTINOPLE

TO

ALEPPO,

AND FROM THENCE

By BAGDAD, and directly acrofs the GREAT DESERT, to

BASSORA.

WITH

Occafional REMARKS on the adjacent Countries,

An ACCOUNT of the different Stages,

And SKETCHES of the feveral Routes on four Copper Plates.

By JAMES CAPPER, Efq;

HÆC DUM INCIPIAS, GRAVIA SUNT,
DUMQUE IGNORES: UBI COGNORIS, FACILIA.

TERENCE.

The Third Edition, with Alterations and Additions.

LONDON:

Printed for W. FADEN, Geographer to the KING, *Charing Crofs*
J. ROBSON, in *New Bond Street*; and R. SEWELL, in *Cornhill*.

MDCCLXXXV.

T O

EDWARD COTSFORD, Eſq; M. P.

THIS WORK IS INSCRIBED,

AS A SMALL TRIBUTE

O F

RESPECT AND ESTEEM,

B Y

HIS SINCERE FRIEND,

AND HUMBLE SERVANT,

JAMES CAPPER.

ADVERTISEMENT.

The principal inducement with
the Author for publishing the first edition of this
work, he does not scruple to acknowledge was to submit to Government, The East-India Company, and The
Public, his reasons for wishing to see revived a dor-
mant plan of sending dispatches to and from India, by
the Red Sea : whether his humble remonstrances have
been ~~attended to~~ so as to promote the prosecution of
this plan may hereafter appear ; but besides this de-
sirable object, he had also in view the pleasure of affording useful information to any of his friends, who
might have occasion to pass to and from Europe, by
the great desert ; and in this part of his design he is
happy to find, he has in many instances succeeded.
The work however in its original form, containing
only instructions for passing through France or Italy
to the Levant, being limited and imperfect ; he has
been constantly endeavouring to procure an account
of the rout through Vienna, and Constantinople, to
Aleppo by land ; which to many travellers may be
far more agreeable, than going any part of the way
by sea.

After

ADVERTISEMENT.

*After much enquiry he has at length been favoured
with two journals kept by Mr. Baldwin lately agent
to the East-India Company at Cairo, who went at
different times from Constantinople to Vienna, and
also from Constantinople to Aleppo*. This gentleman's
extensive knowledge of the Oriental languages, and
his long residence among the Turks, and Arabs,
will no doubt give great weight to his observations on their manners, and customs. The reader
will also find in these additional pages, many curious
remarks and amusing anecdotes; which serve to cha-
racterize the different nations through which Mr.
Baldwin passed: and also many useful geographical observations on classic ground, once well inhabited, and
resorted to as the seat of the arts and sciences; but which
for many ages past, has been little frequented by Europeans. The journals are published nearly in Mr.
Baldwin's own words; they were written in haste,
to convey information to other travellers, and with
no idea of presenting a finished piece of composition
to the public—Ornari, res ipsa negat, contenta do-
ceri.*

---

* When the late rupture broke out with France, this gentleman who was then at Cairo, sent the earliest intelligence of it to
India; which enabled the government at Madras to take Pondicherry before reinforcements could arrive from Europe, or the
island of Mauritius. A proof at once of his merit, and of the
advantage of being able to send dispatches by that rout.

To

ADVERTISEMENT.

To the sketches in the former editions of this work, are added two others, the one, the façade of an ancient monument found in Natolia; the other, a chart of the Red Sea. Much pains have been taken to decipher the inscription still remaining on the building, but in vain; however it is generally supposed to be a mixture of Greek and Phœnician characters. From the necessary size of the Chart of the Red Sea, little more can be expected, than a general knowledge of the relative situation of the places referred to in the work; and those are laid down with all the accuracy possible, in a chart on so small a scale.

PREFACE.

THE indulgent reception the firſt edition of this work met with, makes me
lament that I am called upon for a
ſecond, before I have leiſure to execute
it in a manner more deſerving the attention of the public: but as it is not
unlikely many travellers may in the
courſe of this year have occaſion to paſs
to and from India by land, and be de-
ſirous of profiting by theſe inſtructions,

I have

I have therefore printed off a few copies with some typographical and other neceffary corrections; and having before touched but flightly on the neceffity of opening a communication with India by the Red Sea, I fhall in this preface enter more minutely into the confideration of that important fubject.

Our extenfive and valuable poffeffions in the Eaft Indies have long excited the envy of all the other European nations; nor is it in the leaft improbable that the maritime powers of France, Spain, and Holland, were prompted to take an active part againft us in the late unhappy war, not only with a view to deprive us of our Colonies in the Weft, but alfo if poffible, to tear from us and divide between them, our poffeffions in the Eaft: and that even the Emperor, and Ruffia, Denmark, and Sweden, remained.

mained neuter, in hopes some time or other of at least sharing with us the profits of that beneficial trade. The Emperor principally for this purpose has already opened the Port of Trieste, and is endeavouring to revive the long lost trade of the different cities of the Netherlands. Russia has obtained free egress into the Black Sea, in order to divert into its old channel, that branch of it that was carried on by the Gulph of Persia. Denmark may look forward towards extending their present possessions in that part of the world; and Sweden probably hopes to come in for a share of the spoils, and to obtain some establishment in India by the means of their old allies the French. Had not some ideas of this nature prevailed, we should not during the late war have fought against such an host of enemies,

nor

nor when threatened with deftruction
have been deferted by our beft friends.

THE fame caufes very likely gave
rife to, and may continue to keep alive
the unnatural connection between the
court of Verfailles, and the republican
party in Holland. The French, when
they are rich enough to begin another
conteft with us, are moft undoubtedly
determined to make their attack in the
Eaft; and as they have no port nearer
to the Peninfula of India, than the ifland
of Mauritius, they have formed a clofe
connection with the Dutch, that they
may at once derive aid from the co-ope-
ration of their joint forces, and enjoy
the benefit of Trincomaley, one of the
fafeft harbours in the world; and by far
the beft fituated of any in India, either
for covering their own fettlements in
the Bay of Bengal, or for annoying ours.

Nor

Nor is it furprizing that the Dutch fhould readily join in this plan, for in cafe of a rupture with them, we might otherwife, by means of a fuperior fleet, in a very few weeks drive them off the peninfula of India; and alfo obtain pof-feffion of the ifland of Ceylon, by far the moft precious jewel belonging to the republic in the Eaft.

During the late war we frequently in India had no intelligence from Eng-land for eight or nine months; nor did we hear of the rupture with Spain until upwards of eleven months after the com-mencement . of hoftilities in Europe. The Spaniards fortunately for us, being flow in their deliberations, and by no means quick in their operations, took no advantage of our want of informa-tion: but fhould a war break out with France and Holland, which for the
reafons

reafons I have already mentioned appears to me by no means improbable, we may find all our fettlements invefted before we know they are in danger of being attacked, and hear of their being totally loft, before we are able to relieve them. The means by which we may prevent our enemies anticipating us in fending advices to India, are in fome meafure already pointed out in the introduction to this work; but fince the publication of the former edition, an occurrence has happened that will greatly facilitate the plan therein propofed of applying for a revocation of the Turkifh edict, and which likewife ought to induce them to let our couriers pafs unmolefted through Egypt.

THE occurrence to which I allude is, the treaty of peace lately concluded between the Ruffians and the Turks; by which

which the former have obtained leave in future to pafs the Dardanelles, and to enjoy the free navigation of the Black Sea. After having thus opened the principal door of their empire to their avowed and formidable rivals, they cannot with any propriety or fhew of reafon, refufe us leave at leaft to fend pacquet boats up the Red Sea to Suez; in one cafe they give up a folid advantage, in the other, nothing is afked of them that can even indirectly affect either their honour or intereft. And indeed it may be well worth their confideration, whether it will not be better for them to throw open all their ports to the other Europeans in general, than by partially fharing the profits of their trade with the Ruffians, ftrengthen and enrich that particular nation, of whofe encreafe of wealth and power they have moft reafon to be jealous.

THE

THE Egyptian government being in a great meafure independent of the Porte, it may alfo be neceffary to confider whether the Beys would approve of our couriers paffing through their country. The Beys have always encouraged the trade from India to Suez, as much as fuch a fluctuating and turbulent body of men can be fuppofed to encourage any meafure of public utility. The reafon of which is obvious; if they by any means could bring the India trade directly to Suez, they would receive all the import and export duties now paid at Gedda, to the amount of near two hundred thoufand pounds per annum; and therefore of courfe they will encourage a meafure from which they would derive fuch confiderable profits. The only oppofition we fhould meet with, would come from the Sherreef of Mecca; and even he, as I have before

obferved,

obferved, will no longer be troublefome when he finds that we refrain from trading, and ftrictly confine ourfelves to fending pacquet boats with letters.

ALMOST every year fome event occurs to fhew the neceffity of our being able to fend pacquets by the Red Sea; of which I fhall mention a very ftriking inftance that happened at the conclufion of the laft war. When the peace was figned, the news of it was tranfmitted to India, both acrofs the great defert, and alfo round the Cape of Good Hope; neverthelefs it did not reach Madras until the end of the month of June. On the 13th and 25th of that month there were two engagements by land, and about the fame time one by fea, in which there fell eighty officers, and upwards of two thoufand men. Now had this paffage to Suez been open at

that

that time, the difpatches might have been fent from England to the fcene of action in feventy days, and of courfe have prevented this unneceffary facrifice of fo many gallant men. But this misfortune, great as it was, might have been ftill worfe; for after our fleet bore away for Madras, Monf. de Suffrein propofed to land all his marines and a body of feamen to join the French troops at Cuddalore, and make a defperate attack on our camp. If therefore, the difpatches had by any unforefeen accident been detained only a few days longer, and this plan had been carried into execution, the effufion of blood at leaft would have been ftill more confiderable: nor is it improbable that with fuch a fuperior force they might have cut off our whole army, then lying before Cuddalore, in confequence of which Madras and indeed all our fettlements on the

coaft

coaſt of Choromandel muſt inevitably have fallen into the hands of Tippo Sahib, who would have paid little or no regard to our peace with the French. The fall of Bombay, and Bengal, with their dependencies, muſt ſoon have followed that of Madras; and the loſs of all our poſſeſſions in the eaſt would no doubt have ſhaken the foundations of public credit at home. When it is conſidered then, that the lives of thouſands, the ſafety of our ſettlements, and almoſt the exiſtence of public credit, depend on our being able to convey intelligence expeditiouſly to India; it will naturally be ſuppoſed, that nothing leſs than the fear of incurring an intolerable expence, can be thought an admiſſible objection againſt forming a regular plan for that purpoſe and inſtantly carrying it into execution: but in fact there is no room for ſuch an objection; for the payment of a moderate

rate poftage would more than defray the whole of the expence; which at all events in an affair of fuch magnitude, ought only to be deemed a fecondary confideration.

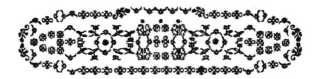

INTRODUCTION.

THE following letter was written in India at the requeſt of Sir Eyre Coote, who once had thoughts of returning to Europe by the way of Suez. It was not at that time intended for publication, however ſince my return to England many of my friends having deſired a copy of it, to avoid the trouble of tranſcribing it myſelf, or the expence of having it tranſcribed by others, I have at laſt reluctantly conſented to its going to the preſs.

D   THIS

THIS the firſt difficulty ſurmounted, I ſhall now endeavour to make this publication as acceptable as I can, by adding to it an account of the proper time, and moſt agreeable manner, of going from Europe to India by Suez : but firſt, as the Turks have at preſent forbidden any Europeans to paſs that way, it will be proper to explain the cauſe of this prohibition ; and to ſhew that their objections againſt travellers going through Egypt may be eaſily removed.

THIS route to India was once the moſt frequented of any, but after the diſcovery of the paſſage round the Cape of Good Hope, it was neglected by moſt European nations, and almoſt entirely abandoned to the Mahomedans, who carry on the trade of the Red Sea in the following manner.

IN the months of November, December, and January, the Mahomedan Pilgrims who are going to Mecca from the coaſts of Barbary, Turkey, Tartary, and Egypt, aſſemble near Suez ; ſome of them form a caravan and proceed from thence by land, but thoſe who have merchandize, freight large ſhips from ſix to twelve
hundred

hundred tons to carry them and their goods to
Gedda, a fea-port within fixty miles of Mecca,
and about two degrees fouth of the Tropic.
As different winds prevail on the different fides
of the Tropic in the Red Sea, fhips may come
to Gedda from oppofite points at the fame feafon
of the year; thofe which come from Suez at the
above-mentioned time, benefit by the N. W.
wind, while thofe that come from India and
Arabia Felix are affifted by the regular S. W.
Monfoon. The pilgrims from the Weft and
North having fulfilled the duties of their religion, and fettled their worldly concerns; contrive if they can to embark at Gedda, time
enough to avail themfelves of the * Khumfeen
wind, which blows foutherly from the end of
March to the middle of May, and conveys them
in lefs than a month back again to Suez: the
veffels from India muft alfo quit Gedda fo as to
be out of the ftreights of Babelmandel before
the end of Auguft. This meeting of the Mahomedans at Gedda has given rife to a fort of annual
fair there, which as all goods imported pay a

---

* KHUMSEEN or Khumfoon, the Arabic term fifty; from
this wind blowing during that number of days in the manner
above defcribed.

regular

regular duty of ten per cent. muſt yield a conſiderable revenue to the government.

THE government of Gedda properly ſpeaking is veſted in the Sherreef or high Prieſt of Mecca; but in order when neceſſary to obtain the protection and ſupport of the Turks, he alſo allows the * Grand Signior to ſend a Baſhaw there. The Sherreef appropriates the major part of the revenues to his own uſe, giving only a ſmall ſhare of them to the Baſhaw; but ſometimes he is obliged alſo to tranſmit a few purſes to Conſtantinople, to keep the Grand Signior and his miniſters in good humour.

IN the year 1774 the Governor General of Bengal propoſed to ſome merchants in Calcutta to ſend a ſhip to the Red Sea, loaded with a proper aſſortment of goods for the Turkiſh markets; and inſtead of landing them at Gedda, he adviſed their being ſent directly to Suez; by which means he expected to eſtabliſh a new trade equally beneficial to us and to the Turks

---

* THE Grand Signior affects to have imperial authority over the three Arabias, and the coaſt of Barbary, but which in fact is never allowed by the Princes of any of thoſe countries, unleſs when it ſuits their convenience as in this inſtance.

in

in general, and alfo to open a new channel for tranfmitting intelligence backwards and forwards, between India and Europe. It is not neceffary in this place to confider the merits of the commercial part of this plan, fuffice it to fay, that the Sherreef of Mecca very foon took the alarm, and ufed all his influence both fpiritual and temporal to put a ftop to its continuance. In his negociation at the Porte in this bufinefs, he was zealoufly affifted alfo by a large body of Turkifh merchants, who were apprehenfive of fuffering by the prices of India goods being lowered in their markets, which muft have totally put an end to the old eftablifhed trade of Baffora and Aleppo. By fuch a weighty concurrence of intereft an edict was obtained from the Grand Signior, which ftripped of its official tautology, and oriental hyperbole, contains no more than what follows.

" HISTORIANS inform us, that the Chrif-
" tians, an enterprizing and artful race, have
" from the earlieft times conftantly made ufe of
" deceit and violence to effect their ambitious
" purpofes. Under the difguife of merchants
" they formerly introduced themfelves into
" Damafcus and Jerufalem; in the fame man-
" ner

" ner they have fince obtained a footing in
" Hindoftan, where the Englifh have redu d
" the inhabitants to flavery; fo now likewife
" encouraged by the Beys, the fame people have
" lately attempted to infinuate themfelves into
" Egypt, with a view no doubt as foon as they
" have made maps of the country, and taken
" plans of the fortifications, to attempt the
" conqueft of it.

" In order to counteract thefe their danger-
" ous defigns, on firft hearing of their proceed-
" ings, we enjoined their Ambaffador to write
" to his court defiring their veffels might not
" be allowed to frequent the port of Suez;
" which requifition having been fully complied ·
" with, if any of their veffels prefume here-
" after to anchor there, the cargo fhall be con-
" fifcated, and all perfons on board be impri-
" foned, until our further pleafure be known."

If it were neceffary, the Chriftians might
very eafily vindicate themfelves from the afper-
fions contained in this edict, and with great
truth and juftice recriminate upon the Mahomedans; and indeed had not the Grand Signior
been ftrangely mifinformed concerning the proceedings

ceedings of both parties in India, he would hardly have ventured to make a comparison between them.

THEY are both equally strangers in that Country. The Mahomedans unprovoked by the Hindoos invaded and took possession of their country; whereas the English introduced themselves as merchants, and carried on a trade very profitable to the natives for upwards of an hundred years, without ever shewing the least hostile disposition against either the peaceable Hindoos, or the Mahomedan usurpers. But after Surage ul Dowla had exercised the most wanton cruelty on the Company's servants, by causing a number of them to be suffocated in the black hole of Calcutta; to revenge their deaths, and to preserve our commercial privileges which we held by grant from the Court of Delhi, we first took up arms in Bengal : nor can the most rigid moralist and much less the Grand Signior find any cause to censure our conduct in thus vindicating the honour and interest of our country*. It is true that Hindostan has been

---

* THE different conduct of the Christians and Mahomedans in India will appear in a more striking point of view from the relation

been more impoverished under our government in the short space of thirty years, than it
was under that of the Moguls, in the course
of three or four centuries; from whence people
hastily conclude, that the Hindoos have been
more oppressed by us, than they were by their
former conquerors. This opinion however is
by no means well founded: it must be remem-

relation of an anecdote of Oriental history, which accidentally
came to the knowledge of the author.

" Surace ul Dowla was the grandson of the great Alyverdi
Khan, who had a favourite wife, a woman of extraordinary abilities and great virtue. When Alyverdi was dying, knowing
the flighty and tyrannical disposition of his grandson, whom
he intended for his successor, he advised him on all important
occasions after his death to consult the old queen, whose
discernment would enable her to foresee dangers imperceptible
to an impetuous and inexperienced youth like him.

When Surage ul Dowla instigated by avarice intended to
attack Calcutta, he consulted this oracle, who advised him
against it in the following prophetic words. " The English are
a peaceable and industrious people; like bees, if properly encouraged and protected, they will bring you honey, but beware of
disturbing the hive! you may perhaps destroy a few of them, but
in the end believe me, they will sting you to death." A pre-
diction which was soon after verified. From this well-known fact
it appears that we were considered as pacifically inclined, and by
no means suspected of a disposition to enslave the natives or
quarrel with the Mahomedans; until compelled to take up
arms to avoid being enslaved ourselves."

bered

b.. .. ..at the Mahomedan invaders fettled in Hind..ftan, and confequently the money their Viceroys exacted from the Inhabitants of courfe returned again into general circulation; and during that time alfo the European nations imported annually large fums in fpecie. But fince we acquired territorial poffeffions, not only ourfelves but alfo almoft all other maritime powers of Europe, have traded with the fpecie of India, which having been for many years paft thus regularly drained, without receiving its ufual fupplies, is now almoft entirely exhaufted. Much more might be urged in our favour againft the charges exhibited againft us by the Grand Signior; but it being foreign to the fubject of this work, I fhall content myfelf with obferving, that his majefty evidently declares in his edict the fentiments of others and not his own; for did he really think as unfavourably of us as he affects to do in order to juftify his conduct, he would not only exclude us from the port of Suez, but alfo compel us to leave every other part of his dominions; whereas on the contrary it is well-known, that he allows us to have factories at Conftantinople, Smyrna, Aleppo, and many other places in Turky, without fhewing the leaft apprehenfion of our feizing on

E

his

his cities, or enflaving his people. We may therefore reasonably confider the Sherreef of Mecca, as the principal author of this fcurrilous libel, who hoped thereby to keep the trade of the Red Sea in its old channel.

WHEN our government thought proper to comply with the requifition of the Porte concerning the trade to Suez, it is much to be lamented, that our minifter at Conftantinople, was not inftructed to ftipulate for fome delay in iffuing the edict, fo that a proper time might be allowed for fending a copy of it to India: for want of this precaution, fome merchants going in the mean time from Suez to Cairo, were plundered and murdered by a body of Arabs. Suppofing even for a moment, what was not the cafe, that the merchants had been informed of the prohibition; ftill they were not punifhed in a regular manner, nor even according to the tenor of the firmaun, which decrees only a confifcation of their property, and an imprifonment of their perfons: whereas thefe unfortunate men were fome of them cut to pieces, and others left to perifh of hunger and thirft on the Defert; a mode of punifhment which plainly fhews, that the maffacre was made by a ban-

ditti

ditti set on by a ruffian like themselves; the Turkish government, despotic as it is, would have proceeded with more regularity, and less cruelty. But here again we may trace the hand of the Sherreef of Mecca, who, no doubt, expected by an act of uncommon violence and barbarity, to deter every other Christian from passing that way; and also at once to gratify his avarice and resentment, by seizing on such a valuable booty.

But the Grand Signior having issued this firmaun, forbidding our ships to come to Suez, and expressed himself in it, in such very strong terms: it may perhaps be deemed expedient to abandon the trade, rather than involve ourselves in a dispute with him; but surely no person will think, that we ought also to give up the right of sending pacquets that way, to which neither the Grand Signior, nor even the Sherreef of Mecca himself, can offer the smallest reasonable objection.

Every man acquainted with India must know, that it is of the highest importance to individuals, to the company, and to the nation at large, to have this channel of communication

E 2   opened

opened again. During the latter part of the late war, after the firmaun was iſſued, the French regularly tranſmitted advices by Suez, to and from India, by which means they frequently anticipated us in intelligence, and of courſe counteracted our operations. It is not neceſſary to particularize every inſtance, but it will doubtleſs be well remembered, that the news of the unfortunate defeat of Colonel Baillie came to England through France, where it was known in February; time enough for them to ſend out reinforcements to Hyder Ally, before the beſt ſeaſon for paſſing the Cape of Good Hope was elapſed: whilſt we who were ignorant of that diſaſter until April, could not ſend out any ſhips before the return of the enſuing ſeaſon, near ſix months afterwards.

SINCE then, nothing leſs than the exiſtence of our ſettlements in India, may ſome time or other depend upon our poſſeſſing a right of paſſing unmoleſted through Egypt; and the prohibitory firmaun was only intended to prevent the trade of Gedda from being transferred to Suez; ſurely no time ſhould be loſt in demanding another firmaun explanatory of the firſt, and declaring that no perſons dependent

on,

on, or connected with the Turkish government, shall impede or molest any British subject in passing up the Red Sea, or through Egypt,
provided they have nothing but papers and such
baggage only as travellers may be supposed to
have occasion for on such a journey. The
Sherreef of Mecca may probably at first oppose
our enjoying this privilege, in which also it is
likely he will be secretly supported by the
French*; but can it be thought prudent in us
to submit to the controul of the one, or to be
dupes of the secret machinations of the other,
especially when consistently with justice, we
can easily get the better of both.

AFTER shewing from what cause, the oppo-
sition to our having a free passage this way to
India arose, and exposing the futility of the
charges contained in the edict: I shall next
consider what is the best time for setting out
from England.

* It is not intended to insinuate that the French ever did, or
ever would co-operate with the Sherreef in employing assassins;
but as our rivals in politics, it is very natural to suppose they
will endeavour to prevail on the Grand Signior, not to revoke
his present firmaun, the existence of which is so disgraceful and
detrimental to us,

THE

THE feafon for undertaking this journey commences early in April, and ends early in June;
during which time a perfon accuftomed to travel,
will eafily arrive at Alexandria from London in
about a month, that is fuppofing he has previoufly determined what route to purfue to the
Mediterranean; and alfo has caufed a veffel to
be prepared for him on his arrival at the place
where he intends to embark. The northerly
and wefterly winds prevail in the Mediterranean
in May, June and July; and therefore in thefe
months, the paffage from Marfeilles, Leghorn,
or Venice to Alexandria, in a tolerable good
failing veffel feldom exceeds eighteen days, and
is often performed in ten or twelve; from Alexandria he will eafily get to Suez in eight days;
and from thence to Anjengo is a voyage of
twenty-five days; to Bombay twenty-eight; to
Madras thirty-five; and to Bengal forty; making the journey from England to India, at
the moft feventy-eight days, at the leaft fifty-
nine, and at a medium fixty-eight and a half.
This perhaps to fome people, may appear too
nice a calculation, confidering it is an undertaking dependent upon many accidents of winds
and weather; but in anfwer to this objection it
muft be remembered, that great part of the

voyage is performed within the Tropic, where the winds and weather are perfectly periodical: and even in the Mediterranean where only the winds are variable, they are never known in fummer, to blow long between the S. and E. the only quarter of the compafs unfavourable to the veffels bound from the ports of Italy and France, to the Levant. The manner of performing the principal part of the voyage, that is through Egypt and from thence to India, is in a great meafure explained in the following letter; but in that nothing is mentioned of the European part of the journey.

IT cannot be neceffary to offer much advice to couriers, they of courfe confult only the moft expeditious mode of travelling, without paying the leaft attention to their own private pleafure or convenience. Gentlemen on the contrary, lefs able, or lefs willing to bear fatigue, will wifh to be informed how they may perform this voyage agreeably; at a moderate expence; and without a rifque of injuring their health. The firft thing to be provided is a ftrong fecond-hand poft-chaife, which will coft between thirty and forty pounds: a large trunk before, a fmall one behind, and a chaife

feat

feat will carry as much or more baggage than is neceffary for two gentlemen, and one fervant; allowing each gentleman a Turkifh drefs, two coats, a dozen and half of fhirts, two dozen pair of common, and one dozen pair of filk ftockings, two pair of fhoes, and other neceffaries in the fame proportion. This perhaps may be thought a fcanty allowance; for generally young travellers prepare for their firft excurfion on the continent, as if nothing could be procured out of their own country; whereas experience foon teaches them that they have not occafion for much more baggage than Mr. Sterne carried with him on his fentimental journey. Thofe who are fond of tea, and are nice about the quality of it, as many Englifhmen are, will do well to take two or three pounds with them; for that which they will find in the inns abroad or any where on the way will be rather coarfe and unpalatable. It may alfo be proper to take a few cakes of portable foup to ferve on board a fhip, and even on fhore, particularly in Egypt; to which may be added a bottle or two of the effence of fellery, with which and a little vermicelli or rice, a perfon may prepare a good mefs of foup on the

Defert,

Defert, with the fame fire that ferves the Arabs
to boil their coffee.

With liquor every perfon may fuit himfelf, remembering that either in France or Italy
at the place where he embarks, he may purchafe a great variety of good wines; and at
Alexandria he may procure a frefh fupply,
fhould his fea ftock be exhaufted on his arrival
there. As to medicines it is univerfally allowed
the fewer he is obliged to take the better, ftill
however he fhould confider his conftitution,
and if he is fubject to any particular diforder,
he will do well to confult his phyfician about
carrying with him a fmall quantity of thofe
medicines which he is moft likely to require.
The moft healthy and robuft are not exempt
from accidents, therefore every perfon may take
from England half a dozen papers of James's
powders, and two pounds of bark, which are
cheap, and eafily carried, and befides the former is feldom to be procured fo good in any
foreign country; no perfon however fhould
take or adminifter thefe medicines, without
having previoufly endeavoured to learn in what
cafes, and in what proportions, they may be
given with efficacy and fafety. This advice,

F   efpe-

especially that which relates to culinary matters, may appear trivial to travellers who have been accustomed to go from one post town to another in Europe; but in Asia, where there are no inns, a prudent man although no epicure will do well to guard against being in want of a sufficient supply of wholesome food. The necessity of carrying medicine will hardly be disputed, but neither would I advise any person to undertake crossing the great desert, without learning to bleed and dress slight wounds; by which means he may not only save his own life, or that of a friend, but he will also merely from the reputation of his skill, obtain great respect from the whole caravan. The practice of surgery it is true is disagreeable to those who are not brought up in the profession; but it is still more disagreeable not to be able to administer relief to a fellow creature in distress.

THESE hints being given for providing a carriage, clothes, provision and medicines, some account may next be expected of the expence, but that is at present impossible. If government or the company should hereafter establish pacquet boats between the European ports and

Alex-

Alexandria, and also between Suez and the ports of India, the expence will then be easily ascertained, and considering the length of the voyage, be very moderate. The chaise will sell at the place of embarkation for as much or more than it cost in England; the only expence therefore of the journey through Europe would be the post horses and charges at the inns, amounting to those who like to live well to about fifty pounds; to the Captain of the pacquet to Alexandria, if he finds the table, forty pounds; at Alexandria ten pounds; from thence to Suez forty pounds; at Suez ten pounds; from thence to India sixty pounds; and for contingences forty pounds; making altogether two hundred and fifty pounds, which divided between two, makes one hundred and twenty-five pounds each. But this account of the journey, and the calculation of the expence must be understood to relate only to the outward bound passengers: those who come home will not travel so fast, nor so cheap; for in the first place they will be much longer coming up, than going down the Red Sea, and conse-quently must pay dearer for their passage; and besides the delay and expence of performing

qua-

quarantine muſt come into the account of the return from India to Europe.

* It is ſaid a plan is now in agitation to ſubvert the Turkiſh empire, the ſucceſs of which muſt in a great meaſure depend upon the part we are inclined to take in the conteſt: but ſhould the Imperialiſts and Ruſſians prevail; the deſert between Suez and Cairo may hereafter become the poſt road to India, and Europeans paſs it with as little apprehenſion of danger, as any perſon now feels in performing a journey from London to Paris. But this perhaps to ſome politicians may not be thought a very deſirable event, leſt ſuch a facility of communication between Europe and Aſia, ſhould in the end be detrimental to our India trade. Let ſuch men calculate the expence of ſending goods up the Red Sea to Suez; of landing thoſe goods, and tranſporting them on camels upwards of ſeventy miles to the Nile; of ſending them from Cairo to Alexandria,

---

* Since the publication of the firſt edition of this work, a peace has been concluded between the Ruſſians and the Turks, by which the former have obtained from the latter the free navigation of the Black Sea, and many other conſiderable advantages.

Ro-

Rosetta, or Damietta; and of reimbarking them at one of those places for the European Markets; and they will find that goods sent round the Cape of Good Hope at a proper season, and subject to no expence, or danger of being spoilt on the way, would come at least fifty per cent. cheaper to any market in Europe.

When the Venetians lost the India trade, no violence, no finesse was used to deprive them of it; the trade died away of itself, because the Portugeze and other European nations, passing round the Cape of Good Hope, could by means of the shortness and safety of the voyage, afford to under-sell them in those articles of India commerce which they received only by the more tedious, dangerous, and expensive channel of the Red Sea: But the probability of the danger of the trade by this route becoming prejudicial to ours by the Cape of Good Hope, being admitted in its fullest extent; are we to suppose that other European nations are so blind to their own interest, so strangely ignorant, or so absurdly indolent, as not to discover it, and immediately avail themselves of their knowledge? If goods can realy be brought cheaper from India to Europe that way,

in

in vain shall we attempt to oppose the general
interests of Europe and Asia; the India trade
must in the course of a few years unavoidably
find its way to the easiest and most profitable
channel. He who thinks otherwise, knows
but little of human nature, and still less of the
principles of politics, and trade.

But whether or not the trade by the Red
Sea will materially operate to the prejudice
of that by the Cape of Good Hope, is not at
present the question; nor is it certainly our
business to encourage the experiment: all that
is immediately contended for is the revocation of the firmaun, as far as relates to obtaining a free passage for our couriers through
Egypt, which in common justice cannot be
refused. The tenor of the firmaun essenti-
ally affects our interest, and the language of
it is extremely insulting; nor should it be forgotten that it was issued in the hour of our
deepest distress. Happily the scene is now re-
versed, of which if we are too generous to take
advantage, still however it is to be hoped we
shall at least oblige the Turks to admit our
claims of a free passage through every part of
their dominions.

THE

THE way to India by Baffora is fatiguing, and rather dangerous, and confequently will feldom be taken by choice, or for the bare gratification of curiofity; but as fome of the company's fervants may be obliged to pafs over the great Defert on public bufinefs, I think it incumbent on me to furnifh them with all the information in my power, that they may execute the orders of their employers with fafety and difpatch; and alfo perform the journey with all poffible convenience to themfelves. For this purpofe I fhall fubjoin to this work the copy of a journal I kept when going that route, and as a common itinerary would be very uninterefting to moft readers, I fhall interfperfe in it fome anecdotes and remarks, which I truft will be deemed both amufing and ufeful.

By the feveral ways of the Cape of Good Hope, Suez, and Baffora, we fhall be able to fend difpatches to and from India at all feafons; but being excluded from any one of them, there will be an anxious interval of fome months in every year, when we fhall mutually be ignorant of what is paffing in the different countries. The beft feafon for leaving England, to

go

go by the Cape of Good Hope, commences in November and ends in April; that by Suez commences in April and ends in the middle of June; and that by Baffora will be the beft route all the reft of the year. To have a conftant fucceffion of intelligence eftablifhed almoft as regular as our pofts at home, would be but a very trifling, if any expence; would afford general fatisfaction to every perfon concerned in India affairs; and at the fame time would be productive of innumerable advantages both to Government and the Eaft India company.

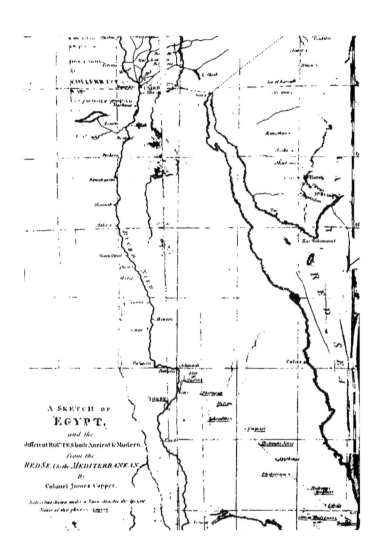

A SKETCH OF
EGYPT,
and the
different ROUTES both Ancient & Modern,
from the
RED SEA to the MEDITERRANEAN.
By
Colonel James Capper.

LETTER.

S I R,

I SHOULD find very little difficulty in writing fuch an account of a journey over land to
Europe by the way of Suez as would be ufeful,
and perhaps in fome degree entertaining to a
perfon who had never paffed over the great
defert; but I confefs myfelf puzzled how to
addrefs you on the fubject, who have already
gone by the way of Baffora, and confequently
muft be perfectly acquainted with almoft every
thing neceffary for a traveller to know. But as

G   I may

I may not be able to difcriminate between what may, and what may not be requifite for you, to know; allow me Sir! to enter on the fubject, as if you had never been in Arabia; the major part of the advice if not neceffary for yourfelf, may hereafter perhaps be ferviceable to fome of your friends.

THE principal objections I have heard mentioned againft a voyage to Europe by the way of Suez are the expence, the inconvenience, and the danger of it. The expence would be trifling to a man of fortune, or when divided between two or three perfons would be lefs to each of them than going round the Cape of Good Hope; the navigation of the Red Sea being now tolerably well known can in a proper feafon no longer be deemed dangerous; and as to inconvenience, I know of none, but what might be almoft entirely removed by means of a little money properly applied. In paffing from Suez to Alexandria, you may poffibly meet with fome difagreeable embarraffments from which a man of rank and fortune is generally exempt in a more civilized country; but moft of thefe are to be avoided, or at leaft greatly leffened by giving

prefents

prefents of no great value to the Beys, and other leading men in Egypt.

In all Arabian and Turkifh countries, efpecially in thofe near the city of Mecca, to avoid the infults of the lower clafs of people, an European fhould allow his beard and whifkers to grow, and always wear an Eaftern drefs; it is beft to make up a coarfe one in the Arabian fafhion for travelling, and another rather elegant in the Turkifh fafhion to wear at Cairo, and Alexandria. If you perform the journey in winter, a pellis will be both ufeful and ornamental; but it may be proper to remark that a Chriftian fhould not wear green clothes at any place in the Levant, for green is a colour deemed facred to thofe who have made the pilgrimage to Mecca, and to the defcendants of the Prophet; nor do the Turks like to. fee an European in red, which was alfo Mahomed's favourite colour.

Those who undertake long journies in Europe are obliged to furnifh themfelves with bills of exchange, but on this they are not indifpenfably neceffary; a perfon of character may have credit to any amount the whole way for drafts

upon

upon England or India; but if you do not
choose to be without a sufficient supply of ready
money, you should take with you Venetian chequins, which are very portable, and at the same
time current in all countries between India and
England.

I PRESUME you will find no difficulty in getting an Interpreter to attend you, who speaks
both the Arabic and Turkish languages: the
former is absolutely necessary from the entrance
of the Red Sea to Suez, the latter is mostly used
by all men of distinction in Egypt.

DURING the month of November, at which
time I should propose you to leave Madras, the
voyage round the island of Ceylon is extremely
tedious; I should imagine therefore it would be
more eligible for you to apply to the Government of Bombay, for one or more of the Company's cruizers, to be sent about the middle of
November to Anjengo, the one for yourself,
and another small one for a tender or pilot vessel.
The captain of the ship on which you embark
will of course take care to lay in a sufficient stock
of every kind of provision for your table, but
above all he should be directed to take plenty of

water

water from Bombay, for that on the fouthern
part of the Malabar Coaft is but indifferent, and
the beft to be got in the Red Sea is fcarcely
drinkable. If you travel through the Travancore country with your baggage in the month
of November, which is during the height of the
Monfoon, the rain may fpoil it; your fervants
therefore fhould fet out with it fomewhat ear-
lier: in a good palanquin you yourfelf will be
very little incommoded by the weather, for you
may fleep every night in good Choultries or elfe
in Churches all the way from Pallamcotah to
Anjengo *. A mariner might perhaps advife
you not to fail fo foon as November from the
Malabar coaft; he would fay it was too early
to make the moft expeditious paffage, for that

---

* In the Eaft where there are no inns, they have been obliged
to erect public buildings for the reception of travellers, which
bear different names in different countries; on the coaft of Choromandel they are called Choultries. The above-mentioned
Churches are thofe which the Catholic Miffionaries have prevailed
on the King of Travancore to allow them to build on the fea
coaft of his country; but the good fathers, although indefati-
gable in their duty, have by their zeal rather injured than ferved
the caufe of Chriftianity; for having received the loweft and
moft abandoned outcafts of the country into the bofom of the
church, and not made any other converts; the Chriftians in India with refpect to religion, are univerfally looked upon as the
refufe of all other people.

you

you will be liable to meet with contrary winds
above Gedda. It is true if you are defirous of
making a fhort voyage to Suez you fhould not
think of paffing Gedda before the commence-
ment of the Khumfeen wind; but for my own
part, I fhould not hefitate about fubmitting to
be a few days longer on board a fhip to enjoy
the fatisfaction of travelling through Egypt in
cool weather. · The Khumfeen wind comes
from the fame quarter as the well known Siroco,
and is productive of nearly the fame effects; it
is unpleafant even at fea, and in paffing the
defert would be almoft intolerable. The plague
is alfo apt to break out late in the fpring, and
feldom rages at Cairo violently before March or
April. As your Captain will doubtlefs be an
experienced officer, and likewife be furnifhed
with good charts, it will not be neceffary for
me to trouble you with a nautical memoire; I
fhall therefore only touch very flightly on
marine obfervations, and confine my remarks
to what may principally contribute to your convenience or amufement.

IT is ufual for fhips in the month of November to work up the Malabar coaft by the
affiftance of the land and fea breezes as high as
Porca

Porca or Cochin, and then with the N. E.
wind to ftretch over to the weftward, and make
Calpini and Schulipar two of the Lacadivi's;
after leaving thefe the next land you make is the
ifland of Socotra, which is fituated near the
entrance of the Streights of Babelmandel. The
Arabian or Eaft fhore of thefe ftreights, to
which you approach within a few leagues, affords fome very romantic views; confifting principally of immenfe mountains and high broken
rocks, with the ruins of caftles upon them;
but there are few inhabited towns of any eminence until you have paffed the Ifland of Perim,
which with the cape on the eaftern fhore forms
what the Arabs call Al Bab, or the Gate.

You will lofe very little time by ftopping at
Mocha, which is the firft feaport town on the
eaft coaft of the Red Sea within the gate, where
you may procure all kinds of refrefhments,
particularly plenty of moft excellent grapes.
If your ftock of provifions brought from Bombay fhould not be good, or be nearly exhaufted;
you may purchafe here Abiffynian fheep, which
are exactly the fame as thofe at the Cape of Good
Hope, half a dozen of which will be fufficient to
laft you to Gedda, where you will be able to fup-

ply

ply yourfelf fufficiently with every thing neceffary for the remainder of the voyage, both of a better quality and at a cheaper rate.

THE fheep at Mocha are very dear, being all brought over as an article of trade from the oppofite fhore of Abiffynia: it appears however very extraordinary that the natives of the fouthern part of Arabia Felix who breed the fineft horfes, mules, and affes in the world, fhould neglect to breed fheep, which doubtlefs would thrive very well in the fame paftures; efpecially as mutton and lamb, conftitute a principal part of their own food.

THE view of Mocha from the Sea, will probably induce you to go on fhore there; the houfes, mofques, minarets, and even the walls of the place are white-wafhed, which at a diftance gives an air of neatnefs to the town, but the infide of it you will find by no means correfpond with its external appearance. The Governor will certainly fend you an invitation by the Company's broker to come on fhore; and if you accept of it, I am perfuaded he will receive you with the utmoft refpect. We were introduced to him as common travellers going

to

to Suez, on our way to Europe. On our landing,
he caufed us to be faluted with three guns, and
the mafter of the port gave us coffee at the
gate where we ftopped a few minutes, to wait
the arrival of the Governor's mufick, and alfo
a horfe to be led before each of us: preceded
in this manner, and attended by fome perfons
of rank, we went to the Governor's houfe,
which ftands in the middle of a large fquare,
and is built of rough ftone, and unburnt brick:
we were conducted up two pair of narrow
broken ftairs into his apartments, where he was
feated in a kind of raifed window feat, to command a view of the fea; he rofe when we entered the room, and faluted us very courteoufly
in the manner of the Arabians, by placing his
right hand on his left breaft, and flightly in-
clining his head. After fome general converfa-
tion about our intended journey, which continued about a quarter of an hour, pipes,
fweetmeats and coffee were brought, and at laft
a cenfer to perfume the beard and clothes, the
introduction of which, in all Eaftern countries
as you very well know, Sir, is intended as a hint
for taking leave.

H   If

IF you choose to sleep on shore, the broker will conduct you to a house belonging to the Company, built in the Arabian stile. A gentleman of the Bombay establishment, resided here two or three years as a supra-cargo, or agent, but the plan not answering either to him or his employers, he was recalled; and the Company's business has since in a great measure been transacted by the broker, who is a native of Guzerat, and speaks both English and Moors.

THERE are some few dangerous shoals between Mocha and Gedda, but nothing is to be apprehended from them at this season of the year, when the wind thus far is fair for going to the Northward. The town of Gedda is not particularly worth seeing, and therefore it is better not to go on shore there, for as it is only sixty miles distant from Mecca, a Christian of whatever rank, even although disguised in the country dress, would be liable to disagreeable taunts and insults from the mob, who almost think themselves contaminated with the breath of an unbeliever when so near their holy ground. Your interpreter, or any Mahomedan belong-

ing

ing to your veffel, will be able to get you any thing you may want.

IT is at Gedda that the difagreeable part of the voyage commences, for within a degree or two at moft North of this place you generally lofe the Monfoon, and meet the N. W. Wind, which as I have before obferved prevails above ten months of the year in this part of the Red Sea. The Gedda pilots who make an annual voyage backwards and forwards to Suez, muft of courfe be acquainted with all the ports, and alfo with the winds and currents and appearance of bad weather, &c.—It would therefore be prudent to take one of them to conduct you fafely to Suez; the expence I believe would not exceed thirty pounds, and he may probably fhorten your voyage at leaft a fortnight, or perhaps three weeks, befides leffening the danger.

IT is much to be lamented, that the Captain of the Coventry Frigate, who lately went up the Red Sea, was inadvertently betrayed into a quarrel with the inhabitants of Cofire, a place about fix degrees North of Gedda on the Wef-tern fhore, and only one hundred and twenty miles from the banks of the Nile; a perfon if

he

he could with safety, would at all times choose
to land there in preference to Suez, for the upper part of the Red Sea is the most tedious and
dangerous part of the whole voyage, and besides
Upper Egypt is full of monuments of antiquity.
The ruins of the famous city of Thebes are
within a very few miles of Ghinnah, where
you go to from Cofire; and the banks of the
Nile all the way from thence to Cairo, are covered with valuable remains of ruined cities, of
which Dr. Pococke and Mr. Norden have published very learned and accurate accounts. It
is said that not only the fort, and a number of
houses were destroyed, but also that near six
hundred of the inhabitants were killed. This
account is probably very much exaggerated,
but it is to be feared as a heavy fire was kept up
on the town for upwards of two hours, many
of the people must have fallen, and therefore
at present it is unnecessary to examine more
minutely into this route. I cannot however
conclude this digression without expressing a
hope that some atonement will be made to
them for their losses, which whether they were
attacked justly or not, is absolutely necessary
before any European ought to venture to pass
that way: by way of retaliation they will sacrifice

crifice every one they can get hold of, until some effectual means have been taken to pacify them.

THERE are many large towns on the East side of the Red Sea between Gedda and Suez, but as one Arabian town differs very little from another, after having seen Mocha, it would only be a lofs of time to ftop either at Yambo, or Tor; the former a place of great trade not far from Medina; and the latter a fmall port inhabited principally by pilots, where there are wells of tolerable good water. Tor is about five and thirty miles from Mount Sinai, near to which there is a convent of Greek Chriftians, faid to have been founded by the Emprefs Helena, and dedicated to St. Catherine. If you have any curiofity to fee this convent in all probability by writing to the monks, permiffion might be obtained from the Arabs to pafs unmolefted from Tor; but the Arabs and monks are not always on good terms; the rapacity of the former, the defencelefs ftate of the latter, and the bigotry of both parties, occafion frequent difputes between them. The monks to guard againft any furprife, conftantly keep their doors fhut, and when they have occafion to go

out

out or come in, are drawn up in a basket to one of the windows of the convent, which are not less than forty feet high; but they seldom go out, having every article of provision for their table within their own walls, which are rather more than three quarters of a mile in extent.

THE voyage from * Tor to Suez may easily be performed in one day with a fair wind, but at any rate in five. Immediately as a ship appears in sight of Suez, a boat is sent on board to enquire the purpose of her coming: and the officer generally brings a present from the Governor consisting of a sheep or two, some small flat cakes of bread, a jar of water, and a small quantity of fruit, particularly oranges, which are juicy and of a very delicious flavour. As the messenger is a man of some rank, it is usual to salute him with three guns, and to entertain him with coffee, tobacco, sweetmeats, &c. When he returns on shore he will carry a letter for you to any person at Cairo, and it will be

---

* THE journey from Tor to Gaza is usually performed by the Arabs in five days, but it is not to be attempted by Europeans until we are on perfect good terms with the Sherreef of Mecca, and also with the Sheicks of the neighbouring desert.

for-

forwarded by exprefs the fame evening, together
with an account of your arrival to the principal
Bey of Cairo, who is called Sheick Belled. It
would not be prudent to write any fecrets in the
letter, but you may fend inftructions concerning
your journey, and directions to have a veffel
prepared for you at Alexandria. Your rank you
may conceal or mention as you think proper.
In my opinion fuppofing they have no reafon to
fufpect you of carrying money or jewels to any
great amount, it would be better to make yourfelf known. They may indeed expect prefents
accordingly, but then their attention to you will
alfo be proportioned to your liberality to them;
the difference of expence will be but trifling to
a man of fortune, and the conveniences you will
derive from being thought a perfon of high fta-
tion will be very great. Lord A. Percy who
was at Cairo in the year 1776, appeared there
in his proper character and was treated with
great politenefs; nor if I was well informed,
was there a great difproportion between the
prefents he gave, and thofe he received in return.
A perfon who from neceffity is obliged, or
from difpofition inclined to be a rigid œcono-
mift, fhould not attempt to travel for curiofity
or pleafure in the Levant, where the infolence
and

and bigotry of the natives can only be got the
better of by an appearance of wealth and liberality; fhould bufinefs oblige any one to pafs
that way who is not rich, or indifferent about
expence; he muft do the beft he can, but he
will-do well to lay in a good ftock of patience.
The Governor of Suez is generally one of the
Beys or Lords who compofe the Ariftocracy in
Egypt, his rank of courfe entitles him to fome
attention. If you chufe to vifit him it is only
neceffary to announce your intention the day
before, and to fix the hour you will go on fhore,
and he will doubtlefs receive you with civility.
But as the anfwer of your letter to Cairo will
probably come back in four days at moft, it will
perhaps be better to wait until it arrives: for
the Governor of Suez will not know what reception to give you until he hears from Cairo,
and in the mean time, you may plead ill health
for ftaying on board the fhip.

The moft acceptable prefents you can offer
thefe people are fhort double barrelled filver
mounted guns or piftols, if bell mouthed the
better, china bowls, fmall French gold repeat-
ing watches, fhauls, keemkaubs, or pieces of
muflin. Any of thefe things given to the Governor

vernor of Suez, and some trifle of the same k'nd
to the officer of the customs, who is a servant to
the Grand Signior, and appointed by the Bashaw
at Cairo, will ensure you great respect, and prevent your baggage from being searched and
tumbled. A cautious man or an œconomist
might object to a declaration of your rank, least
your supposed wealth being made known to the
Arabs, should tempt them to attack you in passing the desert; for my own part I do not think
there is any danger of it, and indeed I am convinced there is more risque in subjecting yourself to be discovered by accident, than by pub-
lickly avowing your rank; and declaring that the
purposes of your journey are curiosity and amusement. The present Duke de Lafoens, a Portugueze nobleman, was incognito at Alexandria
nearly at the same time that Lord Percy appeared
there in his proper character, and whilst the latter was allowed to ride on horseback, attended
by guards, and received presents of horses and
other things nearly equivalent to what he gave
to the Beys; an order was issued to arrest the
former, and it was with some difficulty that
assisted by Mr. Baldwin he made his escape on

I board

board a fhip lying at Alexandria*. The Sheick
Belled has great authority over both the Turks
and Arabs, and therefore protected by his guards,
which probably he would fend to efcort you as
foon as he is informed who you are, you would
pafs the Ifthmus of Suez without any danger of
being molefted.

The diftance from Suez to Cairo is not more
than feventy miles, fome people have reprefented
this little journey as very fatiguing and dangerous. I have already given my opinion of the
danger, which with common difcretion I muft
repeat, appears to me perfectly imaginary; and
as to fatigue you may travel in a tukt-rawan or
litter carried by camels or mules, the motion of
which is not very uneafy: thefe machines are
eafily procured at Cairo, but it would be moft
advifeable for you to get one made of bamboo
at Bombay, which would be both light and
commodious, and ferve you both as a travelling
carriage and a tent. Should you not choofe to
be encumbered with a tukt-rawan, nor the Bey

* The Spaniards and Portugueze carry on a kind of perpe-
tual war againft all Mahomedans; which was an additional
reafon for the Bey's intending to imprifon the above-mentioned
nobleman.

fend

fend you a horfe, your agent will be able to
procure you one at Cairo; but at the worft,
you may borrow one of the Arabian guards who
efcort you from Suez, and thefe horfes although
not very handfome, are far from being unpleafant to ride ; their paces are agreeable, and they
are entirely free from vice.

WHEN the day of your departure from Suez
is fixed; you fhould make a large provifion of
bread and ready-drefled meat, fowls, mutton,
&c. the feafon being cold, fuch things will
keep good for three or four days, which is longer than you can well be on the road to Cairo.
Your party will always halt at night, when you
may drefs any thing, if you prefer hot victuals to
cold. There is no water on the defert, and
therefore I would advife you to take a few dozen
bottles in bafkets from the fhip ; for that at
Suez is rather brackifh, and befides the Arabs
carry theirs in fkins, which are not always very
clean.

NOTWITHSTANDING I think there is no
danger of being molefted by the Arabs, efpecially after having taken the precautions I have
already mentioned ; yet to put it paft a doubt,

I would

I would advife you when the paffport comes from Cairo, to fend your baggage forwards a couple of days before you; and when you have heard by exprefs fent back to you that it is advanced about half way to Cairo; unincumbered with a ftring of camels, that move flowly and detain each other, you may then fet out; and without travelling in the heat of the day, arrive yourfelf at moft in eight and forty hours, allowing even a proper time for fleep and refrefhment on the way. The Arabs, unlefs tempted by the hopes of plunder, or provoked by fome act of hoftility, are never guilty of violence to travellers of any denomination; therefore if your baggage paffes unmolefted, which muft ever be the fole object of their attack, your perfon will be perfectly fafe. This journey might be performed with great eafe in eighteen or twenty hours, but then your baggage muft be left behind; nor will you eafily perfuade your efcort to keep up with you at this rate of travelling.

THE face of the country nearly refembles that of the great defert, being barren and deftitute of trees, excepting a few of the Egyptian thorn, bearing a yellow flower. Within about twenty miles of Cairo, you meet with rocks amongft which

which you may find a ftone that refembles pe-
trified wood beautifully variegated. I thought
it fufficiently curious to be taken to Europe;
and therefore carried a few fmall pieces with
me, which were much admired at home.

IT is neceffary to get to Cairo before fun-fet,
at which time the gates are fhut; for if you
arrive five minutes after they are clofed, you
will be obliged to pafs the night very uncom-
fortably in the fuburbs amongft poor Arabian
huts. But independent of this inconvenience it
is very defi.able to be near Cairo about the middle of the day to enjoy one of the moft pleafing
profpects I have ever feen; the beauties of which
perhaps are fomewhat heightened by coming
after a fucceffion of views every one more dreary
and defolate than the other.

WHEN about three miles from Cairo, from
the fummit of an Hill you perceive that city
fituated in a fertile valley, and watered by the
Nile, which meanders at the fide of, and beyond its walls through a rich country as far
as the eye can reach each way. To the S. W.
is an immenfe high rock, at the foot of which
and adjoining to the town is the citadel and palace;

lace; to the N. and N. W. the buildings cover a fpace of at leaft ten or twelve miles in circumference, amongft which are many magnificent tombs and mofques, whofe domes and adjoining columns give a variety to this view, furpaffing even that of the beft built towns in the Catholick countries, where the churches add greatly to the beauty of their external appearance. The weather was rather hazy the day we were on this hill, or I fhould fuppofe we muft alfo have perceived the Pyramids in the back ground of this charming landfcape.

Upon entering the gates of the city you are not ftopt and interrogated as you generally are coming into the towns on the continent of Europe, but your guides conduct you immediately to the houfe of your European correfpondent; and he the next day will fettle with the officers of the cuftoms about your baggage. If they have fealed up your trunks at Suez, as they ufually do, you fhould not fuffer thofe feals to be taken off, or broken; for they may be glad of fuch a pretence for threatening you with the difpleafure of government, in order to demand a confiderable bribe for hufh money: thefe artifices they will be likely enough to practife upon you

if

if you afford them an opportunity, efpecially if
you conceal your name and rank.

THE officers of the cuftoms at Suez fealed up
our trunks, and alfo our pacquets, and in this
manner we carried them to Cairo; but as much
rain fell whijft we were croffing the defert, we
opened our trunks and boxes in order to dry our
cloaths, but above all our papers; not however
without having previoufly confulted a gentleman
at Cairo, concerning the propriety of it. The
next morning when the cuftom-houfe officers
came to examine our baggage, being told of
what we had done, they affected to believe we
had broken the feals to conceal fome prohibited
goods, or at leaft to avoid paying the proper
duties. We might perhaps have been able to
pacify them by means of a little money, but our
friend flighted their menaces, trufting he fhould
get the Sheick Belled to interfere in our behalf;
unfortunately for us he was again deceived, and
in the end this little act of inadvertency coft us
near three hundred pounds, together with no
little anxiety, on account of being detained feveral days at Alexandria by the order of the
Bafhaw.

AFTER

AFTER your arrival at Cairo, I would advife you as well for health as for pleafure, almoft immediately to repair to the hummam or bagnio. The Turkifh manner of bathing is infinitely fuperior to any thing of the kind that is now known, or at leaft practifed in any part of Europe, for even moft of the inhabitants of Italy, once fo famous for the magnificence of their baths, have long neglected this luxurious but falutary cuftom; as fome of your friends may never have feen a Turkifh bagnio, I fhall attempt a defcription of that I ufed, which was one of the common fort, fuch as are to be met with in every city in the Levant.

THE firft room is the undreffing chamber which is lofty and fpacious, about twenty-five feet long, and eighteen wide; near the wall is a kind of bench raifed about two feet from the floor, and about feven or eight feet wide, fo that after bathing a perfon may lie down upon it at full length; the windows are near the top of the room, as well that the wind may not blow upon the bathers when undreffed, as for decency's fake. After undreffing a fervant gives you a napkin to wrap round you, and alfo a pair of flippers, and thus equipped you are

conducted

conducted through a narrow paſſage to the
ſteam room or bath, which is a large round
building of about twenty-five feet diameter
paved with marble, and in the centre of it is a
circular bench where you are ſeated until you
find yourſelf in a profuſe perſpiration; then
your guide or attendant immediately begins rubbing you with his hand covered with a piece of
coarſe ſtuff called Keſſay, and thereby peels off
from the ſkin a kind of ſkurf, which cannot be
moved by waſhing only. When he has rubbed
you a few minutes he conducts you to a ſmall
room, where there is a hot bath about four feet
deep and ten feet ſquare, in which he will offer
to waſh you having his hand covered with a
ſmoother ſtuff than before; or you may have
ſome perfumed ſoap given you to waſh yourſelf:
After you have remained here as long as is
agreeable you are conducted to another little ſide
room, where you find two cocks of water the
one hot and the other cold; which you may
throw over you with a baſon, the water being
tempered to any degree of warmth, or perfectly
cold if you prefer it. This being the laſt ablution, you are then covered with a napkin, and
from hence again conducted to the undreſſing
room, and placed upon the before-mentioned

K   bench

bench with a carpet under you, and being extended upon it at full length, your attendant again offers to rub you dry with napkins. Some people have their nails cut, and also are shampoed *; the Turks generally smoak after bathing and the operation of shampoing; and in about an hour, a few minutes more or less, they commonly dress and go home.

It is to be wished that some able physician would take the trouble of informing us what would be the probable effects of the use of the Turkish baths in England. If we were to judge by a comparison between the endemical disorders of Asia and Europe, we should suppose that the moderate use of the bath might render the gout

---

* Shampoing is variously performed in different countries. The most usual manner is simply pressing the hands and fingers upon the body and limbs, particularly near the extremities, so as to compress, but not to pinch them. This is the general manner practised by the servants of the Asiatics, but the barbers and the guides at the baths make also the joints and even the vertebræ of the back crack by a sudden jerk, which to people unaccustomed to it in their youth, is rather a painful sensation. The Chinese and Malay barbers particularly excel in this art, which however is very well known, and generally practised all over Asia, where it is thought a necessary substitute for exercise during the hot weather.

and

and rheumatifm as uncommon in this part of the world, as they are in the other.

· Very few Afiatics are afflicted with thefe complaints, although they eat their meat very highly feafoned with fpices, and ftewed in cla-rified butter; feldom take any exercife, and even many of them fecretly indulge in other excefles, which with us are fuppofed to caufe the gout. Why then may we not allow fome degree of efficacy in warm baths and fhampoing, in throwing off thofe humours, which not being removed, occafion the gout and other chronical diforders amongft us; but my knowledge of thefe matters being very fuperficial, I only hum-bly fuggeft thefe ideas to the faculty for their confideration and opinion: thus much however I can pretend to fay from my own experience, that the warm bath is very refrefhing after un-dergoing violent fatigue. In coming from Suez to Cairo, a journey of feventy miles, I was ex-pofed to very bad weather, for two days and two nights, with no tent or covering but a cloak. On my arrival at my journey's end very much harraffed with fatigue, and benumbed with cold I went into a warm bath, in which having re-mained about half an hour I was perfectly reco-

vered,

vered, and never in my life was in better spirits, or more able to have pursued my journey*.

The

* In the last voyage of Captain Cooke which has been published since this letter was written are the following observations on the custom of shampoing, which with the remarks I have taken the liberty of adding, I am in hopes will amuse the curious reader, and be of service to valetudinarians. Mr. Anderson, in the account of his visit to the King of the island of Tongataboo, vol. i. page 323, Cooke's voyage, observes, " when supper " was over, abundance of cloth was brought for us to sleep on; " but we were a good deal disturbed by a singular instance of " luxury, in which their principal men indulge themselves; " that of being beaten while they were asleep. Two women sat " by Tuttafaihie, and performed this operation, which is called " tooge tooge, by beating briskly on his body and legs with both " fists as on a drum, till he fell asleep; when once the person is " asleep, they abate a little in the strength and quickness of the " beating, but resume it if they observe any appearance of his " awaking. In the morning we found, that Tuttafaihie's wo- " men relieved each other, and went to sleep by turns. In any " other country, it would be supposed, that such a practice " would put an end to all rest, but here it certainly acts as an " opiate, and is a strong proof of what habit may effect." Captain Cooke in the second volume, page 63, informs us, that being by indisposition prevented going to a marai in Attaharoo, he sent Mr. King and Omai, and returned on board his ship attended by Otoo's mother, his three sisters, and eight more women. To use the Captain's own words, he adds, " at first I " thought this numerous train of females came into my boat with " no other view than to get a passage to Matavia, but when they " arrived at the ship they told me they intended passing the night " on board, for the express purpose of undertaking the cure of " the

THE day of your arrival at Cairo you muſt determine whether or not you will viſit the Sheik

" the diſorder I complained of; which was a pain of the rheu-
" matic kind, extending from the hip to the foot. I accepted
" the friendly offer, had a bed ſpread for them upon the cabbin
" floor and ſubmitted myſelf to their directions. I was deſired
" to lay myſelf down amongſt them. Then as many as could
" get round me, *began to ſqueeze me with both hands from head to
" foot*, but more particularly on the parts where the pain was
" lodged, till they made my bones crack, and my fleſh became
" a perfect mummy. In ſhort after undergoing this diſcipline
" about a quarter of an hour, I was glad to get away from them,
" however the operation gave me immediate relief, which en-
" couraged me to ſubmit to another rubbing down before I went
" to bed; and it was ſo effectual, that I found myſelf pretty
" eaſy all the night after. My female phyſicians repeated their
" preſcriptions the next morning before they went aſhore, and
" again in the evening when they returned on board, after
" which I found the pain entirely removed, and the cure being
" perfected, they took their leave of me the following morning.
" This they call *romee*; an operation, which in my opinion far
" exceeds the fleſh bruſh, or any thing of the kind that we may
" uſe externally, it is univerſally practiſed amongſt the iſland-
" ers, being ſometimes performed by the men, but more gene-
" rally by the women. If at any time one appears languid and
" tired, and ſits down by any of them, they immediately begin
" to practiſe the romee upon one's legs, and I have always
" found it to have an exceeding good effect.

In theſe two extracts taken from the voyage of Captain Cooke lately publiſhed, every perſon who has been in India will recog-nize in an inſtant the operation of ſhampoing, which, as I have
already

Sheick Belled, and the Bashaw, which will I
suppose in a great measure depend upon their
own

already said in this work*, is universally practised all over the
East. It is with great pleasure I avail myself of the testimony of
two such respectable witnesses, to shew the existence of this
custom, and also to prove its wonderful efficacy. The manner
described by Mr. Anderson is practised in India as it is in Tongataboo, with this small difference, that the shampoers do not
strike violently with the fists, but gently with the edge of the
hands; nor I confess does it appear extraordinary to me that a
person exhausted with fatigue, should thereby be lulled to rest.
It might equally be thought that noise and motion would keep
children awake, but we know the reverse to be true, for they are
always sung and rocked to sleep, and even sometimes for want
of a cradle the nurses strike them gently on the back with their
open hands, which produces the same effect. We may suppose
the King of Tongataboo had long been used to this indulgence,
and therefore like a person accustomed to opiates, he required a
strong dose; such a one as would disturb, and even hurt an European. The operation described by Captain Cooke is the most
common kind of shampoing, and is that which is preferred by
Europeans in the East, who seldom have recourse to any thing
of that nature, excepting in cases of excessive fatigue, or real
indisposition. If it were necessary, many persons now in England could vouch for the efficacy of shampoing, especially in re-
lieving rheumatic or gouty pains; but what farther testimony
can be necessary after the proof given us by a man exempt from
the errors and fancies of weak minds, and whose veracity it is
impossible to suspect. Possessed of such an incontestible proof of
the fact, it were to be wished that a gentleman of Mr. Anderson's

---

* Vide supra,

pro-

own behaviour, or rather perhaps upon the
character in which you choofe to appear. If
you travel incognito there will be no occafion
for you to go near them ; but in that cafe-you
muft fubmit to the mortification of riding
about on a jack afs, as all Chriftians do excepting thofe who have exprefs permiffion to ufe a
horfe: but as Lord A. Percy, and alfo Lord

profeffional knowledge, and philofophical turn of mind, had
upon the fpot afforded this matter more particular confideration :
as a medical man he probably would have been able to explain
in what manner the operation of fhampoing produced the wonderful effects above defcribed ; and his remarks being introduced
into a work fo univerfally read and admired, would of courfe
have been no lefs univerfally known.

Tнε philofopher who is continually in fearch of materials for
forming an ingenious hypothefis, will naturally catch at this
fimilitude of cuftoms between the natives of the iflands in the
Pacific Ocean, and thofe of the great Eaftern continent, to prove
that the former are certainly defcended from the latter. Without launching out into amufing conjectures and difquifitions, in
which I have not at prefent leifure to indulge myfelf; I fhall
only beg leave to obferve, that if another equipment for difcoveries fhould take place, this curious point might in a great
meafure be afcertained, by fending linguifts in the fhips, who are
acquainted with the Arabic, Malay, Chinefe, and Ruffian languages. By carefully following the courfe thefe different languages have taken, we may trace them to the various channels
into which they have flowed, and confequently by this, one of
the fureft guides, at length trace the people themfelves to the
fountain head from whence they fprung.

Charle-

Charlemont before him were both allowed horfes, your agent no doubt will be able to procure you the fame indulgence; but then as I have already obferved, prefents of fome value will be neceffary both to the Sheick Belled, and the Bafhaw. We were informed it was not neceffary to vifit the Bafhaw, whofe authority in the country they told us was merely nominal; but this to our coft I have already faid we found to be a miftake: for had we paid proper attention to him, or in other words had we waited upon him, and given him a trifling prefent; the affair of opening the pacquets would have been paffed over in filence. To guard you againft the fame inconveniences that we experienced through ignorance of the nature of the Egyptian government, I fhall attempt to give you a general idea of it.

EGYPT is divided into twenty-four provinces, each of which is governed by a Sangiack or Bey: the major part of thefe twenty-four Beys refide at Cairo, where always once a week, and fometimes oftener they fet in council, called by them the Divan: the Sheick Belled is the prefident of the council, and executive member of the government; his office is fomewhat fimi-
lar

lar to that of the Doge of Venice, with rather
more authority, but that indeed depends upon
a variety of circumftances, fuch as whether he
is a man of great abilities and firmnefs himfelf;
whether he is fupported by a large party amongft
his colleagues; and whether or not he is on
good terms with the Bafhaw. When I was at
Cairo the Sheick Belled was rather a weak
man, and owed his fafety to the mutual jealoufy
of two rival Beys nearly of equal power, who
both afpired to his place. The Bafhaw is fent
from the Porte as Viceroy on the part of the
Grand Signior; if he can contrive to fow fedi-
tion amongft the Beys, and fecretly attach
himfelf to the ftrongeft party, whilft he feems
to obferve a ftrict neutrality, he fometimes ac-
quires more influence than even the Sheick
Belled himfelf; but then he muft act with
great care and circumfpection, for fhould his
intrigues be difcovered, and the adverfe party
to his prevail, he certainly will be obliged to
quit the country.

THE manner of his difmiffion is characteriftic
of the gloomy and arbitrary proceedings of this
oriental republic. The Beys having come to a
refolution of fending him away, difpatch a

L   Carra-

Carracoulouck from the Divan or council to his houfe, who approaches the place where the Bafhaw is feated, and having filently turned up the corner of the carpet, abruptly goes away; he is however obliged to carry an order with him, which he puts into his bofom, leaving out a corner of it fo as to be plainly perceived. The name Carracoulouck fignifies a black mef-fenger, for he is dreffed in black, with a fort of bonnet on his head, of the fame colour.

THE Bafhaw never pretends to oppofe this mandate or rather hint from the Divan, know-ing that refiftance would very probably coft him his life. He therefore as foon as poffible retires quietly to Boulako, fituated about two miles and a half to the weftward of Cairo; or when he fufpects a violent degree of refentment againft him, he proceeds to Rofetto, and from thence fails in the firft veffel to Cyprus, where he remains until he hears from Conftantinople.

THE Divan or council of the Beys to keep up appearances with the Porte difpatch a fpecial meffenger to Conftantinople complaining of the mifconduct of the Bafhaw; but the Grand Sig-nior confcious of his inability to fupport his
officer,

officer, takes no other notice of his difmiffion, than in fending another Bafhaw to Cairo, and often impofing a fine on the one who has been difgraced. Such, Sir, is the general outline of this Government, and as it is impoffible for you during your fhort ftay in Egypt, to difcover the fecret intrigues of the ftate, fo as to judge which party predominates, you will perhaps think it moft prudent to be equally attentive to both. On a future occafion when poffeffed of full information, and more leifure, I fhall probably trouble you with fome further obfervations on this extraordinary government, but I fhall conclude the prefent account with a curious trait of their policy, which has no precedent that I know of in any other country whatever.

The children of the Beys cannot inherit either the rank or the property of their fathers, nor even be appointed to any office which it is deemed proper for a Bey to hold. It is true the Divan after the death of a Bey, appropriates a part of his property to the maintenance of his family, but the remainder goes to his cafheef or lieutenant, who generally fucceeds both to his office and eftate. Thefe cafheefs are Georgian or Circaffian flaves, whom the Bey has bought

and

and adopted when young, and of courfe educated with great care and tendernefs, with a view of leaving them grateful guardians to their orphan children. This law was doubtlefs fuggefted to them by their diflike to monarchy and predilection for a republic ; but furely it firft took place during the adminiftration of fome childlefs perfon, or the voice of nature would have fuppreffed the dictates of policy.

THE city of Cairo and its environs as you well know are full of curiofities, but nothing attracted my attention fo much as the infinite variety of people in the public ftreets, and yet I could difcover nothing like an original national character among them. The prefent Egyptians are an heterogeneous mixture of all nations, and having unfortunately retained only the worft features both of the minds and perfons of their anceftors, they are in my opinion become the moft difagreeable and contemptible nation on earth, bearing no more refemblance to the former Egyptians, than the prefent ruins do, to their once magnificent buildings.

WHEN you have fufficiently gratified your curiofity at Cairo you may proceed from thence

to

to Alexandria by land; but you will go with much greater eafe, expedition, and fafety, as far as Rofetto by water. There are two forts of boats on the Nile, the one refembling a Bengal budge-row or barge, and the other fomewhat like a Moor punkey*, but the generality of Egyptian boats are inferior to thofe of Bengal, both with refpect to elegance and accommodation. I took one at Cairo of eighteen oars, in which I arri-ved at Rofetto in thirty hours, about two-thirds of the men conftantly rowing whilft the others flept: the banks of the river are covered with well inhabited towns and villages, but as the natives of this part of the country bear not the beft of characters, and are particularly averfe to Europeans, it will not be prudent to truft yourfelf among them. It is even thought ne-ceffary at night, to carry a light in a paper lan-thorn, under the tilt or deck of the boat, to fhew that you are Europeans, and alert; or thefe pirates will fometimes attack you in hopes of

---

* A Bengal budgerow refembles the barges of the city com-panies; a Moor punkey is a long narrow boat to row with ten or twenty oars; the former is ufed for travelling up and down the great rivers in Bengal, and the provinces to the north of it; the latter is feldom ufed but in coming down with the current, with the affiftance of which, when the river is full, they are fuppofed to go at the rate of ten or twelve miles an hour.

plunder.

plunder. Should you come to an anchor you muft alfo be watchful that they do not fwim off from the fhore, and pilfer fomething out of the boat, at which they are very expert.

THE objections againft going all the way to Alexandria by water, is the furf at the Bogaz or mouth of the river at Rofetto, which renders this part of the voyage rather dangerous. It will therefore be better to go on fhore at Rofetto, and from thence proceed by land, the diftance is about thirty-three miles. Chriftians are allowed to make this journey upon camels or mules, and even upon horfes if they will go to the expence of hiring them. If you fet out from Rofetto about eight o'clock in the evening, you may arrive at Alexandria at day break, which in a moonlight night is the moft agreeable manner of travelling; for you would thereby avoid the heat of the fun, which in the middle of the day even in the winter feafon is very unpleafant.

IN advifing you to travel by night from Rofetto to Alexandria, I do not mean that you fhould depart from Rofetto the night of your arrival, for if you can ftay there you will find
fuffi-

sufficient amusement for a week at least; not that Rosetto itself I believe abounds with antiquities, but there are many modern buildings, in and near the city very well worth seeing. It is a place much respected by the Mahomedans, who say if Mecca was to be taken from them, that the pilgrims who now go thither, would in future visit Rashid, i. e. Rosetto; which opinion is probably founded on a tradition that one of Mahomed's nearest relations, formerly lived, and is now buried at a mosque which is situated at the North part of the suburbs. The length of this city is near two miles but it is not more than half a mile broad. In the environs of it are many country houses belonging to Christian merchants whose gardens abound with exceeding fine Oranges, and many of the choicest fruits of the East: but what contributes most to make it an agreeable residence to them, is the liberality and politeness of the Mahomedan inhabitants, who notwithstanding the reputed sanctity of the place, are particularly civil to the Christians; whereas at Damietta, which is situated only on the opposite, or pelusian side of the Delta, an European cannot appear without a certainty of being insulted. For this violent antipathy no other reason can be assigned, but

that

that during the crufades confiderable detach-
ments of the Chriftian armies ufed to land there,
and the accounts of the ravages they committed
being tranfmitted to pofterity, has fixed a deep
rooted refentment in the minds of the Damiet-
tans, that will never be eradicated as long as
thofe ftories are remembered.

EUROPEAN travellers in general complain of
the ill treatment they meet with in all the
countries of the Levant, but particularly when
they are examining the ruins of ancient cities:
the jealoufy fhewn by the Mahomedans on
thefe occafions is always imputed to religious
prejudices, or the want of urbanity; but I fhall
beg leave to account for it in another manner.

IT is generally believed by them that all
Europeans are deeply verfed in the abftrufe and
occult fciences, which makes them confider us
in the fame light, as the vulgar and ignorant in
Europe confider our fortune tellers or conjurors;
that is with a kind of admiration, mixed with
fear, and deteftation. Added to this prejudice,
they are alfo thoroughly perfuaded from the
ftories they daily hear repeated out of the Arabian Nights Entertainments, that there are
many

many fubterraneous palaces in their country
full of pearls and diamonds, in fearch of which
they fuppofe the Europeans are come to Eg? :t :
we always acknowledge that we are look:ng
after curiofities, which ferves to confirm them
in their error; for as they have not the moft
diftant idea of what we mean by curiofities,
they naturally conclude we are looking for the
pearls and diamonds fuppofed to be concealed
in thofe fame palaces; which opinion alfo is
ftrongly corroborated by the zeal and anxiety
fhewn by our antiquarians in their refearches.

As the mean heat of a country is faid to be
nearly afcertained by the mean heat of the
fprings; fo are the genius and charaƈter of a
nation difcovered by perufing their favorite
books; for which reafon I advife you by all
means to perufe thefe Arabian Nights Entertainments before you fet out on your journey.
Believe me Sir! they contain much curious
and ufeful information. They are by many
people erroneoufly fuppofed to be a fpurious
produƈtion, and are therefore flighted in a manner they do not deferve. They were written as
I have already hinted by an Arabian, and are
univerfally read, and admired throughout Afia.

M   by

by all ranks of men, both old and young:
confidered therefore as an original work; defcrip-
tive as they are, of the manners and cuftoms of
the Eaft in general, and alfo of the genius and
character of the Arabians in particular; they
furely muft be thought to merit the attention
of the curious: nor are they in my opinion
entirely deftitute of merit in other refpects,
for although the extravagance of fome of the
ftories is carried too far, yet on the whole one
cannot help admiring the fancy and invention
of the author, in ftriking out fuch a variety of
pleafing incidents: pleafing I call them, becaufe they have frequently afforded me much
amufement, nor do I envy any man his feelings,
who is above being pleafed with them; but
before any perfon pofitively decides upon the
merit of thefe books, he fhould be eye witnefs
of the effect they produce on thofe who beft
underftand them. I have more than once feen
the Arabians on the defert fetting round a fire
liftening to thefe ftories with fuch attention
and pleafure, as totally to forget the fatigue
and hardfhip with which an inftant before they
were entirely overcome. In fhort Sir! not to
dwell any longer on this fubject, they are in
the fame eftimation all over Afia, that the adventures

ventures of Don Quixote are in Spain; and I am perfuaded no man of any genius or tafte, would think of making the tour of that country, without previoufly reading the works of Cervantes.

About half way between Rofetto and Alexandria you come to a place called Madhia, where at flood tide you muft crofs over in a ferry boat, but at the ebb you eafily pafs over on horfeback: near the ferry is a ferai or refting place where you can fleep, but fhould it be neceffary for you to pafs a night on the road, you had better go to the town of Aboukeer, which is fituated on the fea coaft, about a mile and a half to the N. W. of the ferry, for the ferai is open to the weather, and alfo extremely dirty: from Aboukeer, or the ferry, to Alexandria is about feventeen miles.

With refpect to a defcription of Alexandria and its environs, I fhall beg leave as before to refer you to Pococke, Norden, and Neibuhr, &c. taking the liberty however in fome few points to differ from them; and likewife to add fome obfervations that I have not met with in

either,

either of the abovementioned writers, concerning the prefent and alfo the former ftate of Egypt.

THE Mole of about one thoufand yards in length which was built to form a communication with the ifland of Pharos does not appear to me to have been taken fufficient notice of by any perfon. As Alexandria was built with a view to commerce, this mole, notwithftanding fome appearances of gothic work in the arches, is probably coeval with the foundation of the city. Of what excellent materials then muft it have been originally compofed to have refifted the beating of the wind and waves for near two thoufand years! Dr. Pococke with great reafon admires the arched cifterns under the houfes for the reception of the water of the Nile, of which however there are not more than five or fix remaining at this time; but in my opinion the fame labour and expence would have been better beftowed in lining the canal from the Nile to Alexandria, with the fame durable materials as thofe of the Mole; by means of which the city to the end of time would have been amply fupplied with water; and goods with great eafe have been tranfported to it, from all parts of Egypt. For want of being lined the banks of the Califch

OF

or canal are now fallen in, which is one of the
principal caufes of the decline of the trade, and
of courfe of the ruin of the city.

IT has long been a favourite opinion amongft
the learned, both ancients and moderns, that the
Egyptians were acquainted with the arts and
fciences, when all the other people were in a
ftate of ignorance. We are told they difcovered
geometry in making the divifions of land, after
the annual overflowing of the Nile; that the
clearnefs of their atmofphere enabled them to
make aftronomical obfervations fooner than
other people; and that the fertility of their
country gave rife to trade, by enabling them to
fupply all their neighbours with corn and other
neceffaries of life. Thefe arguments are however more fpecious than true, for if we owe the
difcovery of geometry to the overflowing of the
Nile, of aftronomy to the clearnefs of the atmofphere, and of trade to the fertility of the
foil; in that part of Hindoftan which is within
the tropic, there are ftill larger rivers which
overflow annually, a clearer fky, and a more
fertile foil. The Nile only once a year affords
a fupply of water to the countries on its banks,
and the fmall quantity of rain that falls there at
other

other times, does not furnifh moifture enough to keep up the fmalleft degree of vegetation. Whereas the rivers in Hindoftan, particularly thofe on the coaft of Choromandel, are regularly filled with water twice a year, firft from the rains which fall in June, July and Auguft, in the Balagat mountains, where the fources of thofe rivers lie; and afterwards from the N. E. monfoon or rainy feafon, which continues on the Choromandel coaft during the months of October, November, and December. With refpect to the goodnefs of the climate, or the clearnefs of the atmofphere for the purpofes of aftronomy, there can be no comparifon between Egypt and Hindoftan; for at night during the greater part of the year in Hindoftan there is fcarcely a cloud to be feen in the fky, and the air efpecially in the fouthern countries is never difagreeably cold; fo that an aftronomer would have every opportunity and inducement to purfue his ftudies in the open air: whereas, in Egypt the fky is often cloudy, and the air fo cold as to make it unpleafant to be out of doors after fun-fet.

The Indians had alfo evidently the advantage of the Egyptians with refpect to cloathing,
which

which is one of the neceffaries, or at leaft one
of the comforts of life; for if we fuppofe men
firft cloathed themfelves in the fkins of animals,
India abounds in vaft forefts or extenfive fertile
plains, where animals of all kind both favage
and tame, muft have bred infinitely fafter than
in the barren deferts of upper Egypt; but in a
hot country the natives would naturally prefer
garments made of woven cotton. Now, the
cotton fhrub is very rare in Egypt, even at this
time, and it is well known to have grown in
India, and to have been fabricated into cloth,
ever fince we have had any acquaintance with
that country. From thefe premifes, therefore,
it is natural to fuppofe, that the Indians in the
early ages were much more likely to fupply the
Egyptians with neceffaries and comforts of life,
than to be fupplied by them; that the Indians
would at leaft have as much occafion for geometry as the Egyptians; and that they had at
leaft equal if not greater advantages for purfu-
ing the ftudy of aftronomy. Thus far however
all is but conjecture, for we have no tradition
or hiftory of thofe times, when either the
Egyptians or the Indians were in an uncivilized
ftate; but if we purfue the fubject we fhall find
very evident proofs that when an intercourfe
did

did take place between them; that the Egyptians received from Hindoftan all thofe articles of luxury, which the Greeks and Romans purchafed again from them. It would be both tedious and unneceffary to enumerate all thefe, I fhall therefore content myfelf with particularizing filk, fpices, pearls, diamonds, and other precious ftones.

It was formerly fuppofed that moft of thefe articles came from Arabia Felix, but this error has long fince been exploded. It is now well known they were none of them the produce of Arabia, but were brought thither by veffels from India, and from thence were carried up the Red Sea, with other productions of that country.

It may perhaps be objected, that the Egyptians and the Arabians are generally fuppofed to have known the art of navigation before the Indians, and of courfe that although India may produce fpices, &c. the Egyptians and Arabians went thither to fetch them. Hiftory being entirely filent on this fubject we can only endeavour to afcertain this matter, by ftating the arguments on both fides the queftion.

In

In all probability before any intercourfe fubfifted between the Indians and Egyptians, both
people knew how to conftruct fmall boats or
rather rafts for croffing deep rivers, and even
for tranfporting themfelves by water from one
place to another in the fame country; but at
the fame time it muft be allowed that the
Indians had much better materials for building
both fmall and large boats than either the
Egyptians, or even the Arabians; and the boats
of the prefent day plainly fhew in what manner the Indians made ufe of thefe materials.
The planks are made of a light boyant pliant
wood, fewed together with coir or the rind of
the cocoa nut made into a kind of fmall cord;
all the larger ropes are made of the fame materials, and even the oars themfelves are formed
of one ftrait pole with a piece of flat board tied
upon it with a coir ftring to form the blade of
the oar. The prefent large country boats of
forty and fifty tons, efpecially thofe belonging
to the Lacidivi and Maldivi iflands are ftill
built in the fame manner, with no other difference than being on a larger fcale: with thefe
in a fair feafon they make voyages many degrees
out of fight of land; yet nothing of the kind
not even the firft effays of the art could have

N   been

been more rude than thefe now are. It is highly probable therefore that as foon as they knew the latitude of the ftreights of Babel-mandel, and were furnifhed with inftruments for making obfervations, they ventured to pafs over from the Malabar coaft to that of Arabia.

I MAY perhaps be afked when and how it was they became acquainted with the latitude of thefe ftreights? that is a difficulty I believe no perfon can folve any more than myfelf, but it is poffible that there was once a chain of iflands nearly in fight of each other, from the Malabar coaft to that of Arabia, moft of which may have been fwallowed up in fome great con-vulfion of nature, fo as to leave no remains ex-cepting the ifland of Socotra and thofe of La-cidivi and Maldivi: but even fuppofing no fuch iflands to have exifted, ftill furely as the Indians had good materials for building veffels, and a fea to fail upon that is governed by regular currents and periodical winds, neither of which the Egyptians had; we may rather fuppofe that the produce of Hindoftan was carried to Egypt by the Indians, than that it was fetched away from thence by the Egyptians.

If

IF the Indians required nothing from the Egyptians either of the neceffaries or comforts of life; if the Egyptians got fpices and other articles of luxury from India; and if the natives of India were firft acquainted with the fcience of aftronomy and the arts of navigation, all of which I think are probable: it is but reafonable to fuppofe that the arts and fciences were firft known in India, and from thence were brought up the Red Sea to Egypt.

I AM well aware that the advocates for Egypt will call upon me to produce any remains of antiquity in India fo ancient as the Pyramids. To thefe gentlemen I fhall oppofe one impoffibility to another, by afking them to trace back the building of Gour, which feven hundred and thirty years before Chrift was the capital of Bengal; or of the better known Palibothra of the ancients, which was the capital of India, long before Alexander's time. As a further proof that the natives of Hindoftan were in an advanced ftate of civilization near two thoufand years ago, I fhall alfo beg leave to obferve that a plate of copper was lately dug up at Mongheer, engraved with Shanfcrit characters which contains a conveyance or grant of

N 2   land

land from Bickeram Geet Raja of Bengal to one
of his subjects, and dated near one hundred
years before the Christian æra. To enter into
a long detail of reasoning upon this plate cannot be necessary; I am persuaded Sir, you will
in an instant conceive how long the arts and
sciences must have been known in Hindostan,
before these regular divisions of land took place,
and the grants of them were engraved on copper in such characters as would not disgrace our
most skilful artists even at this time.

THE ingenious Mr. Halhed in the preface of
his Bengal grammar, informs us that the Raja
of Kishnagur, who he says, is by far the most
learned and able antiquary, that Bengal has produced within this century, positively affirms
that he has in his own possession Shanscrit
books, which give an account of a communication formerly subsisting between India and
Egypt, wherein the Egyptians are constantly
described as disciples, and not as instructors of
the Indians; and as seeking that liberal educa-
tion, and those sciences in Hindostan, which
none of their own countrymen had sufficient
knowledge to impart. This evidence of the
learned Raja has great weight with me, especially

cially as there are books now extant in Bengal,
written in the Shanſcrit language, which are
copies of others ſaid by the Bramins to be dated
more than two thouſand two hundred years before the Chriſtian æra. This faƈt admitted,
and I firmly believe it very poſſible to be proved,
the Egyptians muſt appear a modern people in
compariſon with the natives of Hindoſtan; for
when the former were advanced no further in
literature, than the conſtruƈting of hieroglyphicks, the latter were maſters of books written in a language which had then attained a
great degree of perfeƈtion.

But this is not all that may be urged in favour of the claims of the Indians, ſome further
proofs will appear upon examining the general
ſtate of commerce at that time all over the globe.
In Europe it was very trifling, of America we
were totally ignorant; and only a corner of Af-
rica was known; conſequently whatever commerce then exiſted muſt have come from Aſia.
About this time there was a chain, or if I may
be allowed the expreſſion, a ſtreet of magnificent
cities from Coptos to Alexandria, which continued in a flouriſhing ſtate, notwithſtanding
the Egyptian empire frequently changed its
Sove-

Sovereign. Nor from any information I am master of, can I find those cities began to decline until the followers of Mahomed transferred the India trade from upper Egypt to the opposite coast of the Red Sea; then, and not before, Upper Egypt became what it still continues to be, an uninhabited desert. If these facts be true, and I believe they will not be disputed; we may reasonably infer from them, that these cities of Upper Egypt not only existed by the support they derived from that trade; but also that they owed their original existence to it. Nor is it Egypt only that has experienced these effects of the India trade; whatever nation has possessed the largest share of it, has invariably for the time enjoyed also the largest portion of wealth and power; and when deprived of it, sunk again almost into their original obscurity.

WHEN the folly of the crusades was over, and the remembrance of the injuries sustained on both sides in some measure mutually forgotten; the Mahomedans intent only on conquest and spreading the doctrines of their prophet, allowed the Christians to carry on the trade between Europe and the Levant, which consisted principally in transporting the India goods from the

ports of Syria, Paleſtine, and Egypt, to thoſe
of Italy. It is well known that the Venetians
for a long time engroſſed the greater part of this
trade, and whilſt they enjoyed it were the richeſt
and moſt powerful people in Europe; we may
alſo trace it from Venice to the Hans towns by
the cities to which it gave riſe in Germany.
But at length the Portugueze diſcovered the
paſſage round the Cape of Good Hope, which
carried a part of the India trade into another
channel; immediately Venice declined, and
Portugal became one of the greateſt nations in
Europe. They however enjoyed their ſuperi-
ority but a ſhort time, for the enterprizing and
induſtrious natives of Holland found their way
round the Cape of Good Hope, and very ſoon
eſtabliſhed themſelves in India on the ruin of
the Portugueze. Whilſt the riches of India
flowed into Holland, the Dutch diſputed the
empire of the ſeas with the united fleets of England and France. At laſt we obtained a larger
portion of this trade than ever was enjoyed by
any nation whatever, excepting the Egyptians,
and every perſon knows at that period Great
Britain gave law to all Europe. Nor does it
require the gift of prophecy to be able to fore-
tell, that deprived of this ſource of wealth we
shall

fhall fiuk almoſt as low in the political ſcale of Europe, as either Holland, Portugal, Venice, or even Egypt itſelf. In ſhort, to ſum up the whole of this argument in a few words. If the arts and ſciences conducted by commerce can be traced back from the weſt of Europe to Italy, from thence to Greece, and ſo on eaſt-ward to Egypt : if India poſſeſſed many natural advantages over Egypt for the production of every article of trade, and alſo for the diſcovery and improvement of every branch of the ma-thematics : and above all, if we have every reaſon to ſuppoſe that the Shanſcrit or original Indian language had acquired a great degree of perfection, and was written with great regula-rity, when the Egyptians were only acquainted with the hieroglyphicks: it is but reaſonable to conclude, that the arts and ſciences came by the means of commerce from India to Egypt, in the ſame manner, as they afterwards came from Egypt to Europe. From the weſt part of Europe they have paſſed over to America, where probably they will ſtill continue to purſue the ſame courſe, until they have finiſhed their circuit round the globe, by opening a communication between the two great continents from the weſt of Ame-rica, to the Eaſt coaſts of Aſia. The further

con-

confideration of this fubject would lead me into a long train of political reflections, I fhall therefore quit it, and return to what relates to Egypt.

THERE are great difputes amongft the moderns concerning the exact fituation of the ancient city of Berenice, on the weft coaft of the Red Sea; and alfo whether or not, there was a navigable canal between that city and Coptos, on the banks of the Nile. If you have leifure to go into Upper Egypt, or can land at Cofire, you perhaps will be glad to know what has been already faid on this fubject, and alfo to receive any information I can afford you, concerning that or any other navigable canal between the Red Sea and the Nile.

BOTH ancient and modern geographers defcribe the remains of a canal from Suez, to a fmall lake of brackifh water about thirty miles to the north of that place; and from thence to a canal faid to have been dug by the order of the Emperor Trajan, which goes from that lake into the Nile a few miles below the city of Cairo: for my own part, I muft acknowledge, I faw nothing like a canal near Suez, excepting

O   a fmall

a small water course, many of which are to be seen both in the great and little desert. With respect to that said to have been cut between Berenice and Coptos in the latitude of twenty-six in Upper Egypt, I think there is reason to doubt its existence. Mr. D'Anville seems to think that a road only was made from the Nile to the Red Sea, and that the mistake arose from there being a navigable canal between Coptos and the Nile, from which it was distant only seven miles. But this great geographer not having entered so minutely into this subject, as perhaps you may think it deserves; I shall offer a few words to your consideration in confirmation of his opinion.

THOSE writers who have placed a navigable canal, or a road between the Nile and the Red Sea from modern Ghinna to Cosire; have probably guessed that it must have been in that situation, because it is the shortest distance from the sea to the river, being in a strait line at most one hundred and twenty miles. But admitting any such canal to have existed in Upper Egypt, of which there are no traces to be found; it is not very likely it should be cut in that direction; for Cosire being almost three degrees beyond the

Tropic,

Tropic, the voyage from the Tropic to Cofire, would to the ancients in their ill-conftructed veffels have been practicable during only the continuance of the Khumfeen wind, which as I have before obferved blows for about fifty days in the year: furely then had the Egyptians attempted to make fuch a navigable canal, they would have made it further to the fouthward, near the Tropic, where it would have been ferviceable to them for fix months in the year; that is, fomewhere near to the fpot where Ptolemy and others have placed the ancient city of Berenice. Dr. Pococke, who does not feem to have adverted to this circumftance of the N. W. wind prevailing fo long below Cofire; thinks that Ptolemy is miftaken in his latitude of Berenice, becaufe Strabo who had vifited Upper Egypt, places Berenice near Coptos; the word near however being only a relative term, may equally mean one hundred, or two hundred and fifty-eight miles; and therefore cannot be deemed any proof that Berenice fhould have been exactly in the fame parallel of latitude with Coptos. The fituation of Coptos is not difputed; and as Ptolemy, and many of the moft refpectable geographers have made the diftance from thence to Berenice near two hundred and fifty-eight

O 2 miles,

miles, moſt perſons perhaps, will be of opinion
that Berenice was ſituated in what is called Foul
Bay, to the ſouthward of Cape Noſe, and within a few miles of the Tropic. Ptolemy Phila-
delphus made a road from the one city to the
other, in which he cauſed wells to be dug, and
what would now in the Eaſt be called Caravan-
faries to be erected; but of which I have been
informed no veſtiges are now viſible. This road
has alſo by ſome people been miſtaken for a
canal; but I ſhall offer ſome objections to your
conſideration againſt the probability of any canal having been made between this part of the
Nile, and the Red Sea.

THE canal muſt have been ſupplied with water either from the river, or from the ſea. If
from the river, ſuch a diſcharge from that body
of water muſt even in the beſt ſeaſon have deprived Lower Egypt of too large a quantity of
this only ſource of its fertility: and in a dry
ſeaſon, which happens at leaſt every fourth or
fifth year, muſt have occaſioned a famine; for
as I have before mentioned the rain never falls
there in ſufficient abundance to keep up the
ſmalleſt degree of vegetation.

IF

IF the canal was to be fupplied with water from the Red Sea, an extraordinary fpring tide, or a ftorm might have broken down the locks, and thereby overflowed Lower Egypt, fo as to render it a mere falt-water lake : but at leaft the mixture of the falt with the frefh water would have made it unfit for the purpofes of hufbandry, and befides the major part of the inhabitants have no other frefh water than what comes from the Nile. If then the Egyptians could not cut a canal without ruining their country, or depriving themfelves of a requifite fupply of water for domeftic ufes, we may reafonably conclude they never would have made the attempt and thereby expatriated themfelves. Thus Sir! having made all the obfervations on Egypt that occur to me, or at leaft fuch as will come within the narrow compafs of a letter; I fhall next confider what meafures you muft take to proceed from Alexandria to Europe.

THE time and manner of your departure from Alexandria muft entirely depend upon the plan which you have laid down ; that is, whether you intend to go directly to England ; or whether you propofe to travel leifurely ; and make a tour

of

of pleafure : You will hardly think of going to
Europe all the way by land through Paleſtine,
Syria, Aſia Minor, &c. I ſhall therefore men-
tion what ſteps you are to take in going by ſea.

Your agent will eaſily procure you a veſſel
on freight to carry you to any of the ports in
Europe, which you may have on reaſonable
terms if you will allow them alſo to put a cargo
on board; and it will be no inconvenience to
you, provided you ſpecify the particular port to
which you are bound; and the veſſel is afterwards
put under your orders.

Of all the nations that frequent this port, I
ſhould adviſe you to employ Raguſians. Their
veſſels are ſtrong and well-found; their ſeamen
are ſober, cleanly, and civil; and their republic
is generally at peace with all the different ſtates
of Barbary. Next to theſe in time of peace, I
ſhould prefer the French, who carry on a conſiderable trade here, and employ in it very large
ſhips; there are but very few Engliſh veſſels,
and theſe are generally ſmall and in bad condition.

It

IF you are in hafte to get home, it is beft to freight the fhip for two months to carry you to any port in the Adriatic or the Mediterranean, and then it will be in your own power to choofe one of thofe places where the quarantine is fhort, viz. Malta, Marfeilles, Ragufa, or Triefte : at all thefe ports with a pattenta netta, or clean bill of health, the confinement is only eighteen days. I would advife you to fteer for Malta; but if the wind comes to the weftward after you have paffed Candia, and before you fee Malta, you fhould then attempt to pafs by the Pharo Meffina in the way to Marfeilles, or elfe to enter the Adriatic and fail for Triefte. When you are advanced up the Adriatic, fhould the wind come round to the N. W. the port of Ragufa will be under your lee; from whence after performing quarantine, you may land in any part of Italy. Before you embark at Alexandria, the Conful who acts as your agent, at the fame time he difpatches the fhip, gives you a feparate certificate or bill of health for yourfelf. If you propofe making a voyage of pleafure without being reftricted in time, and can depart from Alexandria in the month of February, you will of courfe firft vifit the Archipelago; where in the different iflands you will

find

find an inexhauftible fund of amufement. It will be very eafy in the courfe of four months to go to Conftantinople, calling in the way at all the places on the Eaft fide of the Archipelago that are worth feeing; and afterwards when you are going to Italy, to vifit thofe on the Weft. I am extremely forry it is not 'at prefent in my power to give you a particular defcription of all thefe iflands, but at Alexandria you will eafily obtain every kind of information concerning them that you can require. In your return from Conftantinople, after paffing the N. W. end of Candia, if you will wifh to fee the South part of Italy, and the ifland of Sicily, it will be neceffary for you to perform your quarantine at Malta; but as the Sicilians fuffered dreadfully from the plague in the year 1743, I am not certain that you can go from Malta to any part of that ifland, without being detained fome days on board the fhip. At Meffina where the plague raged with its greateft violence, they often impofe a quarantine of feven days, even on thofe who come from the oppofite coaft of Calabria; but the Neapolitans are not fo fcrupulous, therefore having got Pratique from Malta you may land in that city.

THE

THE time spent in visiting Conftantinople and the iflands in the Archipelago, and alfo in performing quarantine, will bring you to Naples in July or Auguft, which indeed is not the moft favorable feafon; but that cannot be avoided, unlefs you prolong your ftay at Conftantinople or the iflands, fo as to arrive at Naples in September or October, which is exactly the plan I fhould moft recommend, for by this little delay, you will have full time to examine countries, which are in the higheft degree worthy of your attention: you will be able to pafs the winter moft agreeably at Naples; and you will have all the following fpring and fummer for your journey through Italy and France to England; the warmth of the fun increafing, as you advance towards the North.

And now Sir! having conducted you to the continent of Europe, I fhall beg leave to conclude; not however without affuring you that if neceffary, I fhall be happy to afford you any further information in my power, and alfo that I am,

  S I R,

   With great refpect,

   Your moft obedient humble fervant,

FORT ST. GEORGE,
Nov. 29, 1780.   JAMES CAPPER.

P

A

J O U R N E Y

F R O M

CONSTANTINOPLE to VIENNA,

B Y

GEORGE BALDWIN, Efq; &c.

WE hired a coach, an old caft-off fiacre, to carry us from Conftantinople to Vienna, with four horfes to draw it; two horfes to carry our baggage, a janizary to protect us, and a ferugee or poft-boy to conduct us. We began the journey on the 28th of September, 1780, upon a Thurfday, from Mr. Willis's houfe in the village of Belgrade; Mr. Willis and his brother Stuart accompanying us part of the way. In eight hours we arrived at ponte Picolo or Cutchuk Chickmagee, and were joined by Dr. Lucci;

we

we lodged in a new conak pretty well accommodated: in fact our bed furniture we carried with us, and it confifted of nothing but a carpet, two fmall fquare cufhions to fet on, and two cufhions to lean or lay our heads on, as our inclination might prompt, and a quilt to cover us. On Friday the 29th of September in the morning we departed; all the way on our journey the fame objects were varied by different afpects; the country hilly on the right, and on our left, the fea. In three hours we arrived at Buyuk Chikmagee or ponte grande, a much pleafanter fituation than ponte Picolo. Breakfafted, and in five hours more got to Silivria, this town which is confiderable, is fituated on the declivity and fummit of a hill, has five mofques, and an ancient Greek church with infcriptions, which the Prieft could not interpret. We remained here till Saturday morning eight o'clock (30th September) when our friends left us. This feparation did not a little difturb us; Mrs. B—— who for the firft time in her life now found herfelf bereaved of all her acquaintance but myfelf, and juft leaving thofe fhe had great reafon to efteem, was totally overwhelmed. The very fine country we paffed had no attractions for her, and gloomy and fad we went

through

through this day's journey, a feven hours march
to Chio Oglu. In this ftate of mind we took
up our lodging at a fpacious and once magnificent conak, when an occurrence happened that
excited our curiofity, a paffion that is not to be
ftifled by affliction. The Devan Effendi of
Wallachia made his appearance with a fuit of a
dozen carriages, and a long cavalcade of more
than an hundred horfes. He is an officer appointed by the Porte to co-officiate with the
prince of Wallachia in caufes wherein Turks
and fubjects are concerned; the fupreme power
being vefted in the prince, who is a Greek, and
appointed by the Porte. This and the princi-
pality of Moldavia are the only veftiges I know
of the ancient Greek dominions; the Greek
language is fpoken at court, and all the inftruments of government are drawn up in that language. On the road from this place, whence
we departed at five o'clock (1ft October) Sunday morning, we met a much more confiderable
train attending the fifter of the reigning prin-
cefs of Wallachia, and related to the druggaman
of the Porte. This dignity fo founding is but
of a precarious tenure, fince the Porte have upon
a late occafion affumed and exercifed the unex-
- ampled prerogative of depofing and beheading
the

the prince. The country is hilly, and well interfperfed with villages and trees, the road good;
we loft fight of the fea on the preceding day.
In ten hours we arrived at Burgas, a large village with a confiderable mofque in it; as yet no
ficknefs on the way, but we heard reports of
the plague raging at Adrianople. The people
were collected at the entrance of the town,
with tents pitched and mufic playing, to celebrate their feftival of Bairam with dancing and
fongs. The Turks faft during the whole moon
of Ramazan, by a ftrict abftinence from meat
or drink, or any thing fenfual, from fun-rife to
fun-fet; but many of them indulge in pleafures
during the night. At the end of the Ramazan,
or rather upon the appearance of the new moon
of Bairam, they celebrate a feftival of three
days, cloathing themfelves entirely new, and
giving into every amufement that a people cha-
racterized for temperance and fobriety may be
fuppofed to indulge in.

WE refted at this conak till five next morning (2d October) and then purfued our journey.
The road is very good and pleafant, but hilly;
on the way for hours together, to the right and
left, we faw fwarms of Locufts, myriads; the
atmof-

atmofphere was darkened with them; it was their coupling time. The male was diftinguifhable, being of a fine yellow colour, and the female of a dark brown. This may be confidered as their laft ftage, they take flight, and falling in their paffage, they depofit their eggs half an inch in the ground, and die. The invincible fuperftition of the Turks in all their metaphyfical tenets, makes them as blind. in their tolerance of this evil, which they could eafily prevent; as they are in neglecting every precaution againft the effects of the plague; but they fay, " What God has decreed, muft be fulfilled." We arrived at Affa at four o'clock in the evening, a village only four hours diftant from Adrianople, or Aderne, as the Turks now call it. No plague here, and from the information our janizary brought us, it had ceafed at Adrianople. Our room was fmall and low, and part of one fide of an old fquare building, having a gallery within, tumbling almoft in its laft ftage of ruin. A mofque ftands in the center of the yard, and near it is a bafon of water furrounded by fome trees, it was juft enough to keep us from the fpleen. As we did not credit the laft accounts we had heard of the plague having ceafed at Adrianople, we confequently determined

mined not to go near it. On Tuefday morning
therefore (3d October) at fun-rife, taking our
departure, we made a tour to a ferry below the
city, and in an hour and a half arrived at Cara-
gatch, the fummer retreat of the French merchants eftablifhed at Adrianople. We were feen
as we entered the village by a Monf. Terraffon,
and conducted by him to his own houfe, the
abode of genuine indifcriminate hofpitality,
even to ftrangers, and thofe of a country hoftile
to his own. The condition of one of our horfes
made it neceffary that we fhould get another,
and retarded us in this place all that day, and
the next. We were vifited by Monf. Meynard,
his mother, fifter, and brother, who expreffed
themfelves concerned that we had not fallen to
their lot; but they made us all dine with them
on Wednefday. Monf. D'Argus alfo would
have vied with his compatriots, if time and his
own misfortunes had not made it impoffible;
enfin, *c'etoit la benediction de Dieu.* They
were as happy as they made us, and I never
was more fo in my life. We were near the
plain of Demftica, and the village of Demirbafh,
renowned in the history of Charles XII. of
Sweden. We walked over this theatre of his
extravagant exploits with a kind of reverential
delight.

delight: now a scene of pastoral tranquillity, scarcely inhabited, and but little heeded.

RETURNING to the village with our amiable party, we were curious to know the nature and object of their settlement at Adrianople. Trade I know to be their pursuit, but we enquired after its foundation and resources. They supply the city and its environs with the various produce of Europe, which is conveyed to them from Constantinople; either directly by land, or from Rhadosto, whither it is conveyed by boats; and from Smyrna by the port of Envi, in the Egean sea, and thence up the river Marizza to Adrianople. Their consumption is considerable, and in return one of their greatest articles of exportation is hare skins, which they buy as a substitute for the Canadian beaver; and send to the number of between three and four hundred thousand annually to France. I was astonished at this surprizing nursery of hares, but the account is certainly founded in truth. Bred in Wallachia and the intermediate tract of land, they are driven in large parties by the severity of the winter, down to the plains: the snow with which the ground is covered betrays their

Q   haunts

haunts to the hunter, and thus they are eafily enfnared.

WE had a view of the city of Adrianople, in which there appears fome magnificent mofques and other public buildings. It extends a confiderable way along the river Marizza, juſt after it has been joined by the Arſa and Tunja, and from thence rifing in a gradual afcent, the greateſt part of the city is feen on an elevation, which impreffes a very advantageous idea of its beauty and importance upon the traveller's mind. The plague was preying at that very time upon the lives of its inhabitants, and forbad our nearer approach. Notwithſtanding we did not go thither ourfelves, we were not free from very well founded apprehenfions of the danger we intended to avoid; for our conductors had been into the city, and in company with the people of it; they had been cautious they faid, but our reliance was in the mercy of Providence.

As we came to a crofs road in the fkirts of the city on our way from Affsa, we faw upon an eminence a man erect upon a ſtake, at the height of three feet at leaſt from the ground;

he

he had been impaled, and was placed there in terrorem to others. It is not a very unufual fight in the dominions of the Turks.

On Thurfday, the 5th of October, we took our leave of Carragatch, but our French friends would attend us part of the way; they muft fee us acrofs a river we had to ford at a danger-cus place; we knew nothing of the river, and therefore a cart upon much higher wheels than our coach being about to pafs, we got into it, and took our baggage with us leaving the coach to follow. We got over dry and fafe, but our coach was nearly loft. Our friends fwam their horfes over with us, and after that inftance of their very cordial attention, and po-litenefs; bid us adieu, and returned. We ftaid to fee them fafe on the other fhore again; made figns of our fatisfaction and gratitude, and went heavily on. We forded and were ferried feve-ral different times in this day's march, which lafted eight hours over a beautiful country, and at length brought us to a Bulgarian village called Hebibchay. We had been joined at Carragatch by two Greek priefts who begged the favour of our protection on their journey to Belgrade, to which we had no objection. We

refted

rested in a Chriftian's hut, nothing more than
mud walls four feet from the ground, and
thatched. We flept here, for the firft time,
on the ground; that is, on our carpet fpread
upon the ground. The language of thefe people is the Bulgar, fomething of the Illyric.
We could not underftand it, all our entertainment therefore was derived from our fight;
the women appear hardy, and do not conceal
themfelves. We made a good fire in our hut,
forgot the humility of our lot, and in defiance
of vermin, paffed the night in fome degree of
comfort.

On Friday at fun-rife (6th October) we left
this place, and paffing over a very fine hilly
country in fight of the river, in eight hours we
arrived at Armanak, where a magnificent khan
was originally built for the accommodation of
the troops, and now affording a fhelter for travellers. We however, after a flight repofe,
continued on to Semiky, a Bulgarian town,
which we reached at fun-fet. The women
flocked to fee Mrs. B——, and viewing her
with a great deal of aftonifhment, I afked one
of them what was the reafon of their wonder?
fhe anfwered, to fee a woman who had never
done

done work. There was so much simplicity and so much ignorance of a state of refinement in this answer, as to dispose us to bear with their importunities. The Bulgarian families intermarry, unite, and make common cause. The custom is for the husband to live in the paternal house of his wife, and their numbers accumulate in some families beyond credibility. We bought a sucking pig for twenty paras, or one shilling; and one of our sacerdotal companions undertook to dress it, as he did also to interpret for us, in which we were sometimes at a loss. We had not discovered all his merit till this day, perhaps not all then. Our bed was again upon the ground.

On Saturday morning at sun-rise (7th October) we renewed our journey, and passing by some villages and over a fine country, arrived at four in the evening, at Papasquoi. This village is situated in the plain of Philipopoli (by the Turks called Phillibey) near a small stream, which makes it pleasant. Our nocturnal accommodation as usual; but the vermin rather more importunate; fatigue however is an irresistable opiate, and we got a proper portion of sleep.

On

ON Sunday at fun-rife (8th October) we renewed our march for Philipopoli; in half an
hour we came in fight of the city, it being
fituated on a rock leading to it over a plain,
the river Marizza meandering by it, and fer-
tilizing and beautifying the country in its way.
Rice grows in great abundance in this plain,
and good in quality. There were numbers of
waggons going to and fro upon the various roads
in the plain; and gave figns of an activity, and
induftry, which is very unufual in the other
parts of the Turkifh dominions. The fact is,
a confiderable iron mine in the neighbourhood,
gives employment to all thefe convoys of waggons, and the character and conftitution of the
people is more fuitable to commerce, than in
the province we were leaving behind us. We
entered Philipopoli at eleven o'clock, and had
to afcend a very narrow and fteep road to the
refidence of Sig. Demetrio Khiro, a Greek,
with whom we took the liberty to fojourn.
This gentleman is a Raija, or Chriftian tributary
of the Grand Signior, but protected by a barat,
or privilege of exemption, allowed to the Am-
baffadors of the Porte. Every Ambaffador is
complimented with the privilege of giving pro-
tections to the number of thirty-two as fervants,

but

but they are fometimes fold to the rich Raijas
for confiderable fums. Signor Khiros's houfe
is fpacious, very pleafantly fituated upon the
fummit of the rock, and commanding a beautiful view of the plain beneath, watered by
three rivers, the Arta, Tunja, and Marizza,
juft as they are approaching to a junction in the
vicinity of Adrianople. Our hoft himfelf was
a confiderable trader in red cotton yarn, which
he fends in large quantities to Ruffia, in leffer
to Germany. There is alfo a large confump-
tion here of India piece goods, fupplied by the
company of Armenians, at Conftantinople;
nor are thefe the only confiderable objects of
fpeculation. We tarried all this day Monday
the 9th of October, and on Tuefday the 10th
at eight o'clock in the morning we refumed our
journey.

One of the hind wheels of our coach had
been newly hooped, and other reparations made
fo as to give us greater confidence in our vehicle
we began to defcend the rock. In iffuing from
the town, we immediately found ourfelves
on a very long bridge over the Marizza, which
having paffed, our way lay between fields of
rice, juft gathering and treading out. In fix
hours

hours we arrived at Bazarjeek, a large town on the plain conspicuous by reason of its mosques and gilded domes, and admirable for the beauty of its situation. We were lodged in the bishop's palace, and from a * Kiosk to the westward, commanded the finest view of a campania without exception in my knowledge, that this country affords. Close under our window ran a gentle stream, and further on united with the main body of the river. Near the junction is a wooden bridge, enlivened by a constant concourse of people on foot or on horse back, and with carriages, incessantly passing and repassing. The view extends over this plain or rather beautiful lawn, which is pleasingly interspersed with clumps of trees, to the foot of the Balkan mountain; thence gradually ascending, and displaying a diversified scene of rustic art and nature, still enchanting to the very top. Near this town is the mine of iron I have spoken of, which is said to be very productive. It is open to the industry of every adventurer, the sultan takes no heed of it; why he permits others to work it, is a mystery to those who know the principles of his government not to be explained; but cer-

* A Turkish summer-house.

tain

tain it is any one may enjoy the fruits of it.
On Wednesday morning (11th October) at sun-
rise we left this town, but the same scene was
before us, we proceeded along the plain, drawing gradually to a Cul de Sac, and in two hours
came to rising grounds, constantly increasing
in acclivity towards the summit, and near the
top growing extremely difficult and steep. At
four in the evening, without any accident,
we reached Palanka, a Turkish village of three
houses, on the summit of the Balkan, and took
our station for the night. Our best choice was
the common stable, and very calmly and con-
tentedly we took up with it; spread our carpet,
and patiently submitted to this hard, but sometimes necessary lot of travellers. Before night
came on however, we amused ourselves with
walking about the hills; observed some vestiges
of an ancient tower, collected some wood for
kindling a fire, and when tired withdrew to
rest. We got over the apparent hardships of
our situation, and at sun-rise were well recruit-
ed for prosecuting our next day's adventures.
Thursday the 12th October, we set off to compleat our passage over the mountain, leaving a
horse behind, worn out with toil. This Balkan, which I have heard so often talked of, as

R   the

the impaffible barrier and defence of the Turkifh dominions in Europe; is, if no better barrier is to be oppofed to the power of their
neareft neighbour, in my opinion, a bad de-
pendence indeed. From the fummit, beginning the defcent, is feen a beautiful meadow,
and about its center a town, with a fingle
mofque in it, called Ifternam. We arrived
there at noon, and dined; but thought fit to
force our march to a village, four hours further,
in order to reach Sophia with more certainty
and eafe, in the courfe of the next day. Our
horfes were the worfe for it, we got however
to Bakreglee, a town in Servia. This place is
fituated among fome oak plantations, upon the
hills, at a diftance from the road. The people
are robuft, and thought rude, but they feem to
poffefs their competency. In departing from
this horde the next morning (Friday 13th Oc-
tóber) we had to defcend a moft rugged and
unbeaten traft of road, and could only have
paffed fafely over it with the affiftance of a
dozen of thefe ruftics, which they readily afforded us. It employed us two hours, when we
were brought in view of the valley of Sophia.
It exhibits a very charming profpect, as the
foil is rich, and covered with a delightful ver-
dure;

dure; feveral villages contribute to adorn the
profpect, and beyond all, the city of Sophia.
The mountain of Vetofa, well known for its
minerals, and the river rifing from its bowels;
make two additional and interefting objects in
this landfcape. When the rains are heavy, a
variety of metallic ores, and often of pure gold,
are brought down by the torrent. A fpring of
hot water runs through the city, and is con-
verted into a bath, for the conveniency of the
inhabitants. Upon converfing with the archi-
mandrite on the fubject of the gold mine, he
affured me, that eight villages gained a conftant
fubfiftence from fifting the fands brought down
by the rains, and frequently were found among
them precious ftones of confiderable value.
Such a treafure offering to the eager avidity of
the Turk, made it a matter of wonder to me,
how the officers of the Porte fhould neglect it;
and begging the prieft to inform me of the
reafon of it, he folved it in the following manner. Their avidity, he faid, refpecting this
matter, was the caufe of their reaping no advantage from it, for the workmen being too
poorly paid for their labour, concealed the
fruits of it, and would take no pains to multiply
their difcoveries. The officers alfo, who were

employed

employed in collecting thefe riches, were too much tempted by the facility of enriching themfelves, to be true to their truft; and reprefenting the deficiences which were caufed by their infidelity, to the poverty of the mine; laid government under the neceffity of abandoning the purfuit. So true it is, that in a matter of firft moment to all governments, and in which the fpirit of Turkifh prerogative can know no bounds, but indulges every fpecies of violence; the want of judgment defeats their aim. No circumftance in the hiftory of Turkifh miniftry, can give fo ftrong a proof of the infufficiency of their fyftem, as this: they cannot gather, where nature has profufely beftowed her gifts; but like true defpots, cut down the tree, to get at the fruit—It is the nature of all defpotifm.

We left Sophia, on Saturday (14th October) at fun-rife, and our journey lay along a fine country, exhibiting all over the face of it, quite to the road fide, an exuberance of wild ftrawberry plants, which owing to the clemency of the feafon, were generally in bloffom. In fix hours we got to Kul Kallah, and halted to recruit our horfes for a march of fix hours farther.

ther. There is a large khan in this place, but decaying faft. We proceeded in an hour, and foon penetrated among the mountains; our road lying through a chafm, apparently formed by fome ftrong convulfion of nature. The road was bad, we therefore could proceed but flowly, and confequently it was late and dark when we arrived at Sari Buroot, where we flept. The next morning, Sunday (15th October) at funrife we departed, and paffed over a hilly country in about four hours to Sharquoi, where we were well entertained. Our room was by the fide of a prifon, where a dozen of gypfies were chained together by the neck; men and women indifcriminately, in order to extort a tribute from them. We refted two hours, and continued our journey over hills, to Ak-Palanka. In this laft ftage we met the courier going to Conftantinople, and were happy by his means, to fend fome tidings of our progrefs to our friends. Our lodging at this place was worfe than ufual, and made us very impatient for the return of day.

On Monday the 16th October at day break we refumed our journey. The firft part of it was over mountains and bad roads to Banaquoi, where

where we dined, and in one hour and a half
more arrived at the bifhop's palace at Nifha.
Another horfe worn out; the other three almoft exhaufted, and requiring reft. The bifhop received us with infinite politenefs and urbanity; wifhed us to ftay a week with him,
and did every thing in his power to engage us
to comply with his requeft. He preffed us to
attend divine fervice the next morning at his
church, promifing to officiate himfelf by way
of giving an air of folemnity to the occafion,
and in every refpect took great pains to entertain and honour us. His name is Maccarius,
nearly allied to the reigning prince of Wallachia. He has travelled into Ruffia and pretends
to a perfect knowledge of the ancient Greek
literature. The women here wear caps in the
fhape of helmets, compofed of quantities of
paras*, ftrung together into that form. This
is the capital of great Servia. We left it on
Wednefday morning (18th October) at eight
o'clock, and in two hours entered the fkirts of
the famous wood of Belgrade: during the courfe
of this day's march, the appearance of the country was fometimes open, fometimes clofed in

* A fmall Turkifh coin.

with

with wood. We dined at Alikſinſa, ſix hours ride from Niſſa, and went four hours further on to Reiſna. The road was tolerably good; but the ſky grew cloudy and threatened us with rain; a circumſtance of all things moſt to be dreaded in the wood, as the roads in that caſe are rendered almoſt impaſſible. We reached Reiſna however before it began, but ſoon after, and during the whole night, it never ceaſed for a moment. We were under a very bad roof, in a large barn or ſtable, in a kind of watch loft, and with the proſpect of being detained there, moſt unpleaſantly ſituated indeed. It cleared up in the morning (Thurſday 19th October) and we ſet off, but the roads were deep, our horſes ſulky, our tackling bad, and every thing croſs. With the utmoſt difficulty, we arrived in ſix hours, after breaking our coach pole, and much of our harneſs, to Parakin; four hours ſhort of the appointed place; where we took up our night's abode: all this while in the wood. The ſky grew ſerene and a ſtrong wind aroſe which continued all night, very much to our advantage, and on Friday morning (20th October) before ſun-riſe, we again purſued our journey. In two hours we reached a town on the river Morva, and ferried over it,

and

and immediately entered the thick of the wood
leading to Zaghadina, where we dined, and
afterwards to Bagherdena, to pafs the night.
This day's journey of eight hours, was over
confiderable hills, covered with lofty oak; but
as the weather proved fine, the journey was not
fo gloomy and difagreeable, as it would otherwife have been. Next morning, Saturday, 21ft
October, we fet off again early, and marched
ftill through the wood to Haffan Bafha Palanka,
where we paffed the night; and on Sunday,
22d October; as early as poffible, proceeded by
Golan and Krotzka to Zweybruchen, where we
flept. On Monday morning, 23d October,
by eleven o'clock, we arrived at Belgrade.
Our janizary had preceded us to get the Bafha's
paffport, for leave to pafs the confines, and
met us by the fide of the Danube, with a Juuk,
prepared to take us acrofs to Semlin. We got
there at about one o'clock the fame day, and
reforted immediately to the place allotted for
our quarantine.

WE had letters of introduction to the Baron
de Sturm, commandant of Semlin; and he and
his lady did us the honour of a vifit the fame
after-

afternoon, offering us every affiftance and in-dulgence, the nature of our confinement would admit of.

SEMLIN is a fmall town, fituated upon the peninfula, between the rivers Danube and Sa-va, juft at the conflux of both, and immediate-ly oppofite the town of Belgrade, which has been the theatre of fome of the great exploits of prince Eugene.

The Lazzaretto or infirmary, is upon a low point of land neareft to the river; having the town at the back of it. The rooms are fuf-ficient for the accommodation of paffengers, but unavoidably damp and unhealthy, they are warmed by ftoves, which make another incon-venience equally intolerable; for the air fo rari-fied by a heat impregnated with the metallic properties of the ftove, fell directly upon our lungs, and nearly fuffocated us; which obliged us to renounce our fires.

THE weather towards the firft part of our time in this place was fine, and we had liberty to make fhort excurfions into the country, in a carriage or on foot, upon promife of obferving

S   the

the ſtricteſt diſtance from all we met, and having a guard to accompany us. We were too eager of this privilege for our good, for walking too far on a cold day, to ſee a fiſhing party; Mrs. B—— was ſeized with an illneſs, which, in its conſequences, embittered our journey the whole way from Semlin to Vienna.

THE Lazzaretto, which is built upon a large ſpot of ground, and is very ſpacious, is generally pretty well filled with merchandize imported from Turky.

DURING our ſtay we were variouſly entertained; a fair was to be held, juſt upon our terminating the quarantine, and people were aſſembled to attend it of all denominations, and from very diſtant parts. There was among the reſt, a company of itinerant merchants, that had wandered from the mountain of Tirrol; uniting at the ſame time, their mercantile and muſical talents, and blending and improving them both for the common good. This company came to our quarters in the lazzaretto, and entertained us with their muſic. A woman accompanied them upon the harp, and the whole party playing upon various inſtruments,
and

and having a good choice of airs gave us compleat satisfaction. It coſt us two florins, and they were ſatisfied.

HAVING performed our three weeks quarantine we were happy to quit immediately the cold and comfortleſs ſituation we were in, for an appartment offered us by the director of the quarantine in his own dwelling. Mrs. B——— had been very ill for ſeveral days with a fever, and was yet in a very critical ſtate. We ſpent a few days in this ſituation with very little ſign of her amendment, and at length reſolved to ſet off. We bought a four-wheeled chaiſe of the director, but the body nothing more than that of a common whiſky, old and impaired in every part of it. We left Semlin in the rain and were from ten o'clock in the morning, till ten at night, creeping and plunging along before we got to a place of ſhelter. We were to have been conveyed in ſix hours to Peterwaradin, and inſtead of that, with joy we put up with a room in a cabaret at Petſche almoſt overflowed with rain. It had a long table in it, ſuch as is found in the moſt wretched of public houſes, and thereon I ſpread our carpet, Mrs. B——— being reduced to make

S 2

it

it her bed for the reft of the night. I for my part laid myfelf down upon the bench by the fide of it, fummoning to my aid all the patience and refignation that was wanted to endure a fituation fo full of complicated diftrefs. We fet out as early as we could next day and arrived at Peterwaradin about twelve o'clock at noon; Mrs. B—— continued very ill, but being houfed at a tolerable auberge, we fent for a phyfician to prefcribe for her. She refted all that day and night, and next morning had fpirits enough to defire to go forward but with the fever ftill upon her, the weather was rather finer and we ventured on. The roads were fo bad it was with difficulty we got along; our way lay for the moft part by the Danube fide. We got to Glofhan where we changed horfes and went on to Kerakatfch; but here they detained us fix hours while the horfes could be got; they were conveying wood for the poft mafter. The weather was fine which heightened our chagrin beyond bearing, and the indifference of the people at the poft houfe almoft drove us to defpair: at length they made their appearance and we got to the next ftage Patfch. We had no long delay here, but our horfes were very unwilling to get on. They carried us

through

through the town, and near a mile beyond it,
but in croffing a bridge of loofe timber laid
acrofs a deep ditch, they turned fo fhort as to
bring one of the hind wheels of our chaife upon
the timber ends, and canted them up, fo as
nearly to overfet us in the ditch. I faw the
danger before we came exactly upon it, and
jumped out with Mrs. B—— juft in time to
efcape the fall. I ftopt the poftilion inftantly,
and by jumping into the ditch, and putting
props under the timber ends, the carriage got
fafe over the bridge and we remounted. We
had not gone far however before our horfes
became reftive, and turning out of the road,
ran us into a bog clofe by the fide of the Danube; every effort to get out for many hours
was vain, but at length with the affiftance of
two additional horfes, and the prefence of the
poft mafter himfelf we got back to the poft
houfe, where the woman of the houfe did all
fhe could to relieve and comfort us. She made
Mrs. B—— fome broth, and gave up her own
bed for the whole night. The next morning
early we were able to proceed, and endeavoured
to recover our chaife and baggage which we
had been obliged to leave fticking in the mud expofed to be plundered by the firft paffenger. We
made

made several attempts to drag the carriage back, but the horses were unequal to it. It had settled at least four feet in the mud, so that we could not move it for several hours. It was Sunday morning, and some very stout peasants, a dozen at least, passing to the town to church, I begged their aid and offered them money: they sat their shoulders to it, and relieved us at once; having got us into the right way again, one of them taking Mrs. B—— into his arms, carried her over the bad road to the carriage. We thanked them as our deliverers, gave them what contented them, and were glad to get on again. We got to Novasella and from thence to Vukovar; we had no provision with us, nor could we ask for any, but by signs; we walked into the post-master's kitchen at Vukovar, though it was otherwise no public house, and there being several pipkins on the fire with soups and stews, we expressed a desire to partake of them. The cook-maid who saw us and understood us very well, was inflexible to our demands; all that we could get of her for an answer was *nix, nix*; I therefore helped myself, and before Mrs. B—— could get the soup to her lips, she fainted in my arms; this scene excited the woman's compassion, and with the

relief

relief she brought, we were in an hour or two,
enabled to proceed. Our next ftage was Effek,
but we had yet to furmount many difficulties:
the way lay over a wide common, and night
coming on, we got out of the road, and went
round, and round, for hours in the fame circle;
at length we heard the found of horfes feet, by
the direction of which, we were once more
put into the high road: about three o'clock
in the morning we got into the town, and
were carried to a lamentable beerhoufe, where
we were glad to find a place of reft. Mrs. B——
had fuffered the utmoft agonies during this
journey, and was apparently breathing her laft.
At day light I fallied forth to get fome affiftance, and the poft-mafter being near, I recom-
mended myfelf to him. He had a good houfe,
and very humanely offered to accommodate me
with a room, and the domeftic comforts that
his family afforded; I very happily embraced
it, and returning to Mrs. B——, took her in
my arms, and removed her to this hofpitable
dwelling. The name of the poft-mafter to
whom we were fo much indebted, was Franco-
laki; I got proper medical advice, and every
other defirable affiftance, and was happy enough,
on the 17th day, to fee the fever which had

never

never intermitted, compleatly diflodged. We were vifited and invited by the commandant of the place; General Mattheifan and feveral of the officers and their ladies, and were enabled in a few days, to leave the place, full of gratitude and admiration of the benevolent treatment and hofpitality of the good people of Eſſek. We exchanged our carriage here, and again purfued our route. The poſt from hence to Vienna are as follows: from Eſſek to Baraniwar, the roads were deep and very bad; next to Siclos, to Funffkirken; to Geofziget, to Iſtvandi, to Babofea, to Prefnitz, to Iharos, to Canifea, to Kahath, to Szala Egeſſek, to Kerment, to Stein, to Am Anger, to Gunz, to Grofwarafdoff, to Edenbourg, to Grofholflein, to Wimpaſſeing, to Hochan, to Vienna.

A

JOURNEY

FROM

CONSTANTINOPLE to ALEPPO,

BY

GEORGE BALDWIN, Esq;

IT is neceſſary to obtain a Firman or order from the Porte before you can be furniſhed with poſt horſes. The method obſerved by Franks (by which appellation all Europeans are diſtinguiſhed in Turky) is to apply to their reſpective miniſter by whoſe direction it is demanded of the Porte, and always granted: but any ſubject of the Empire may obtain it by direct application to the Vizir, and upon paying a fee of three Cruſh and a half (or 7s. 6d.) to the clerk. I obtained mine by this means,

and

and at feven o'clock in the morning of the 11th
of May, 1780, left the Metropolis in a boat,
and croffed the Hellefpont to Scuder, or Scutari,
the Chryfopolis of the ancients.

Mr. —— a painter by profeffion, myfelf,
Selim Aga a Tartar guide, Emin Aga who
begged my efcort; my fervant Matthew, an
Armenian, and two poft boys, called Serugees,
compofed my party. At half paft eight we
mounted, and on our way paffed Malteffa, Fe-
nar, Cartel, and at Bendik we ftopped and re-
frefhed. The Turks have proportioned their
diftance to time, and by my general obfervation,
it turned out about four miles to the hour: in
riding poft through, they often run down three
hours in one. The appearance of the country
to the left, or North Eaft; is a gentle afcent
over hills, leading to the foot of very high
mountains. The foil feems good, is well cultivated, and the vegetation much forwarder, than
in Europe, though at fo fmall a diftance from
it. All the way on our right we had a view of
the fea of Marmora, the princes iflands, the
gulph of Ifmit, the coaft of Mandania, and
mount Olympus. At five o'clock in the evening

ing we arrived at Gheibize, the firft Menzel Khané, or poft houfe from Scuder.

It muft be remarked, that we were all equipped as Tartars, and were from long intercourfe with the Turks, pretty well able to fupport our difguife. We were enjoying our pipes and coffee at this place, and compofed in fact for the evening; but this was to be a journey of adventures, and the arrival of a certain Ofman Aga, on his way from Aleppo to Conftantinople opened the firft fcene.

He brought with him the baggage of an Englifh gentleman, who had accompanied him to the ftage before, but had ftrayed from his party, and might probably, he faid have fallen among thieves, as he had been miffing from two o'clock in the morning. I looked into the baggage to find by fome fuperfcription of letters, who the perfon might be, by which I difcovered him to be a Captain James Smyth. The circumftance engaged one to mount, though tired, to go in fearch of him. We paffed a village after two hours march called Mallum, and further on to a ferry, where we embarked with our horfes, and failed acrofs an arm of the gulph of Nicomedia, courfe fouth eaft, to a low point

T 2

of

of land on the oppofite fhore; diftant only a
quarter of an hour's walk from a hamlet, called
Herſek. This traverſe which we performed in
three quarters of an hour, avoids a fix hour's
round by land, and in winter, is fometimes fo
boiſterous, as to be impaffable for days together.
My firſt buſineſs at this place was to enquire for
my diſtreffed countryman, and I was almoſt inſtantly gratified by finding him in a folitary coffee houſe, extended on a mat afleep; I called to
him by his name. He ſtarted, ſtared, and looked aſtoniſhed, as if he ſtill thought himſelf in
a dream. This gentleman had been in India,
aid de camp to General Egerton, and had arrived thus far on his way to England. He had
been moſt cruelly beaten by the man that
accompanied him acroſs the deſert from Baffora
to Aleppo, and from thence, by colluſion with
his Tartar guide, had forced his company upon
him, in ſpite of all the precaution he had taken
to avoid it. They had travelled difagreeably together as far as Kiz dovréne, but on the road
from this place, which is notorious, I am told,
for robbers; both this man and the guide ſet
upon him, and forced him to fly for fafety to
the woods. He concealed himſelf there till
day light, and then crept into a corn field by the

road

road fide, whence he efpied a hofpitable paffenger, an honeft Boftangee, who conducted him
to the place he was in when I found him. He
little expected when he laid down in this fituation, furrounded by a people he knew nothing
of; and full of apprehenfions of further ill treatment, ignorant of their language, and helplefs
in many other refpects, that he fhould be roufed
by a countryman feeking to relieve him, and
adminifter fuccour to his diftrefs. It appeared
to him, as I faid before, the effect of a dream,
and he was long awake before he could be un-
deceived. When informed of my name, he
knew it, and appeared rejoiced to fee me. It
is flattering to obferve a public prevention in
one's favour! I refcued Mr. Smyth from the
people of Herfek who were unwilling to give
him up; nor till I had threatened to return to
Conftantinople to complain, would they releafe
him. I procured him a boat, and a trufty perfon to attend him, when he had embarked, and
I faw him fet fail for Conftantinople (it was
twelve o'clock at night) I returned to my quarters and laid me down to reft.

At half paft four in the morning (12th May)
I refumed my journey over hills and dales, a

four

four hours ride, to Kiz dovréne. The nightin-
gales, which in this country fing all day, and
are near every fhaded brook, are fo numerous,
and their notes fo fweet; as to make the ride a
fpecies of enchantment. The village we are
now at, is inhabited by Bulgarians, and is fituated on a hill, furrounded by higher hills, and
near the foot of an ancient ruined caftle. Thefe
people are independent, and preferve their original cuftoms. Their women go unveiled, are
free, joçofe, and of a complexion and forward-
nefs, that befpeaks no apprehenfion of infult or
violation. We breakfafted with this Amazo-
nian tribe, upon eggs and milk, and proceeded
on our journey with the fame horfes towards
Chiniflik. The road is the greateft part over
hills, enriched with fpontaneous odoriferous
fhrubs, and pleafant, if excefs can pleafant be,
to the extreme. When you come to the defcent,
the profpect is delightful. On your right appears
a vaft lake, adorned with a rich verdent margin;
in front, at the eaft end of the lake, the city of
Chiniflik; and to the left, promifcuoufly dif-
perfed on rifing grounds, in a femi-circular view,
a variety of villages, beautifully environed by
variegated lands, and cattle brouzing on the
fummit. It was ten o'clock when we reached
the

the city. You enter among some vestiges of a ruined wall, and on a square tower, high up, is seen a Greek inscription: nothing in the town else did I see worth remarking. We got fresh horses, and mounted at four o'clock; our road lay along the middle of a rich valley, and on each side adorned with walnut trees, a small rivulet running between. The cultivation on each side the mountains, to their utmost scope, appearing more extended, and giving a livelier picture of industry; than I had met with in any other part of Turky. After an hour's ride in the valley, we began to ascend the hill to the right, and at the top, were brought in prospect of the Brussa road; only six hours distant from the capital of that name, once the royal residence of the Sultans: it is described by a river running at the foot of it. This river has its source in mount Olympus, and is increased by the hot springs of Brussa, and the dissolving snows from the heights above it. It flows northward to the Black Sea, and enlivened our prospect all the way to Leuke (our third post-house) a city of some note for its manufactures. We did not arrive before ten o'clock at night, fatigued and hungry. We supped on pilo and stewed fowl, our invariable fare, and rested like travellers worn down with fatigue.

fatigue. At four in the morning (13th May) we mounted, and as we rode along the town, could fee the world in motion. Many of the inhabitants are Chriftians, and their houfes fpacious; the river runs at the bottom of the town. Beyond it on the banks, were planted for a long tract, the white mulberry tree, for the nourifhment of filk worms; for in this territory is produced large quantities of filk, which finds its way to Europe, under the denomination of Bruffa filk; and for its goodnefs is in high repute. We paffed a very delightful valley, well watered and interfperfed with trees during the firft part of this poft; and towards the end, over a very fteep and difficult mountain. The road is level on the top for a good ftretch, but we foon came to a fhed occupied by a guard, who were provided with frefh water, and fuch fruit as the fituation would enable them to procure, for the convenience of the traveller. We met here half a dozen men, whom we fhould have been very forry to have met upon the road : fellows that had been difmiffed from the fervice of the Bafha of Trebizond; and who, in their ftate of dereliction, are known to have recourfe, for fubfiftence, to every fpecies of violence. It is the cafe all over the Turkifh empire, when any Ba-

fha

ſha is depoſed, his mercenaries are diſcharged, and under the denomination of copſiſſes, or men at leiſure, go a free booting upon the public, until they are reinſtated in ſome other employ; they then plunder for their maſter, for their avocation is to deſpoil. Theſe men eyed us with looks of rapine, but they ſaw us armed; they took the road we came, and we proceeded on our journey. This was a poſt of ten hours to Sekut (fourth poſt-houſe.) Near this place, and in view of it, is buried the firſt of the Ottoman race, the great Ali Oſman Pádeſbá. His tomb appears at about half a mile diſtant from the poſt houſe, by an iron palliſading, and a plantation of lofty cypreſſes. We mounted at five in the afternoon, rode over mountains, and latterly over a fine plain, to Eſkee Shaher (fifth poſt-houſe.) As we were ſeaſoned a little to riding by this time, we accelerated our rate, and performed this poſt in ſeven hours; which brought us in at twelve o'clock at night. Upon the ſofa in the room to which we had been uſhered, lay a Turkiſh guittar, a hum-drum kind of a thing to European ears, but temptation enough to divert Selim from his inclination to reſt. He ſtrung it to his voice, and with an hilarity of ſong, which Yorick would have har-

U   monized

monized to the fineſt feelings, he charmed away
the night. At dawn we ſallied forth to view
the baths; and the morning diſcloſed to us a city
beautifully ſituated on the acclivity of a hill,
commanding a wide expanded view over a fruitful, well watered plain. A copious ſource of
natural hot water riſes in the ſkirts of the city,
and unites its ſtream with a conſiderable river,
flowing to the ſouthward. The baths are built
over the ſpring; but where the waters iſſue, to
the place of their junction with the river, all
along its courſe, the poor inhabitants are employed in great numbers, in ſuch offices of neceſſary and uſeful ablution, as the conveniency
and importance of ſuch a benefit, muſt unavoidably ſuggeſt. I bathed in theſe celebrated hot
baths, and drank of the waters; both were re-
ported to have efficacies conducive to health.
In effect, I can vouch for their property of immediately operating all the good purpoſes of eaſe
and relaxation. I was as delaſſé in half an hour;
as if my ride had been only ten, inſtead of two
hundred miles. It was a fortunate refreſhment,
for we got but indifferent horſes here; but we
made them go notwithſtanding in ten hours,
over hills, and a pleaſanter, becauſe a varied ſoil,
to Saidi Khazzee, (6th poſt-houſe.) This place
is

is diftinguifhed by a large fquare building, with
a magnificent mofque in it, on the top of a hill.
It took its name from a furprizing fanton, who,
by the tradition of the Sheick, moft marvel-
loufly confined a gigantic fpirit, that had done
incredible ravages, and was the terror of the
country round about. The daughter of Soly-
man the Great, had it declared to her in a vifion,
that if fhe would make a pilgrimage to this fpot,
and dedicate upon it, a mofque to the prophet;
the Sheick fhould be endued with power to
fhackle this fpirit, whereby the people fhould
be relieved: all which was regularly complied
with, and fulfilled. The Sheick gave the painter
and myfelf a paper of white powder each (part
of the giant's bones pulverifed, I fuppofe) which
had the property of preferving us againft danger.
We took it and gave him alms, which is the
only valuable property it had in effect. " That
" of drawing from the credulity of the ignorant,
" or the complaifance of the enlightened, a tri-
" bute which contributed to his affluence and
" fupport." We left this place at four in the
afternoon, and becaufe at the next poft-houfe,
the horfes could not be got in from pafture before a delay of ten hours, we croffed the country
directly over mountains and through woods to

U 2   the

the place where they were. We were nine hours, which detained us until one in the morning. Corfaff Basha is the name of the seventh post-house; but we deviated to an itinerant horde. We roused the chief from his cabbin, composed of the trunks of fir trees, laid as they were hewn down, one upon another, in a square figure ten feet high; and covered at top with the branches and leaves: it had a chimney place formed with mud and stone, and a glorious fire in it. We took his place, lighted our pipes, made some coffee, ordered our horses to be got by morning, desired some eggs and milk might be provided for breakfast, and then resigned ourselves to sleep. At day light, Hadgee Mustafa, Menzel Aga of Cofruff Basha, a man of a very respectable appearance joined our party. After some conversation, by which he had discovered that we were Franks, he entertained us with a very unexpected breakfast, for he had his family among the horde, and flocks and herds abounding about him: he told us also of a wondrous building in the neighbourhood of the place, on which Frank characters were inscribed; and which must have been erected, he said, before the Turks had driven the Infidels (Ghiaours) from the country. It was only an hour's ride,

and

AS TVAY ENS AE ELVPONI TIN   KIACARBEPHIAIBDAFTAELEATAKTPAEM   BABA ME MI FALS CRITALO KEVMGTENSLIKEMAACS

and he propofed to lend us horfes and to conduct
us thither. Mr. ——, the painter, and myfelf
mounted, and followed our good old Turk to
this fragment of antiquity. We proceeded over
a hill, and through a wood of pines, to a fmall
valley, in which a rivulet runs, fupplied by water oozing from an ancient aquaduct; and two
hills in the form of fugar loaves, on which are
the ruins of two ancient towers. Thefe were not
the objects our Aga had intimated for our obfervation. He led us further to a ground af-
cending to the foot of a rock, making the extreme
angle of a chain of inferior mountains.   As we
approached, it exhibited a beautiful ornamental
facade, engraved on a polifhed furface of the rock.
It feemed to have been a work antecedent to the
claffical inftitutions in architecture; but regular,
fublime, and bold. On the extreme right margin of the facade, beginning about one fourth of
the height from the ground, and wrote fideways
upwards to about one third of the top, is a clear
and diftinct infcription of ancient characters :
There appears another on the projected cornifh,
over the upper part of the left fide of the facade,
but fome of the characters effaced, the reft very
clear.   I offer no conjecture as to the intentions
of

of their authors; but give the fact, and leave the comment to antiquarians.

THE depth of the rock, for it projects from the great mafs of the mountain, and is palpable on three fides of it, is no more than twenty feet: and appears, excepting the polifhed and engraved facade in its rude, irregular and natural fhape, without a fign of excavation, or the veftige of a building. I had a thought at firft indeed, that, as it faced to the eaft, it might have been a monument of pagan worfhip: but further on, is another in the fame ftyle, of lefs magnitude and beauty, facing the north, which again ftaggered my opinion. I may conclude with fafety, that, let what will be meant by it, it prefents at leaft to the contemplation of the curious, a fingular, magnificent and lafting view of the then ftate of ornamental architecture. The when, and by whom, as before obferved, is left to the decifion of the curious and learned.

IN a line parallel to the facade, northward at about one hundred and fifty paces diftant, is another rock, ifolated, and of a conical form, exhibiting as many cavities of the fame nature with thofe of the catacombs near the pyramids of Egypt, as the folid rock could poffibly contain. I
entered

entered into many, but none communicated with the others. They have all a variety of niches, some more, some lefs, as the number expected to be depofited therein, required the labour of making them; and leave no room to doubt, that they were receptacles for the dead. They are now receptacles for the living, for I found a bird's neft in one of them with feveral young, but I thought there was more piety in leaving them undifturbed, than impiety in difturbing the infenfible dead.

We returned to the hamlet at half paft one in the afternoon, and mounted our horfes at two, very well fatisfied with our digreffion and difcovery. The old man, in the idea which is generally entertained by the inhabitants of the Eaft, that all Franks are doctors or conjurors; held out his pulfe, which I directed to the painter, as having fomething more intenfe in his phiz, to know if he was well. As it generally turns out, that people act from impulfe, and only afk the advice of doctors when they want it; I told Mr. —— to recommend a dofe of rhubarb, with which he was provided, to cool the old man's blood: he faid it was very wife and proper, thanked us, and bid us farewel.

We

WE paſſed through woods and over mountains, three hours march before we got into the high road. Proceeding, we ſaw to the left of us, or north ſide of the road, many cavities in the rocks, of the ſame appearance of thoſe I deſcribed in the laſt ſtage; but leading one into the other to infinity. The entrance to theſe caverns is ſmall, but ſome of them may be capable of containing three hundred horſe. Further on ſtands a rock, ſingly, and of a ſugar-loaf form, excavated and diſpoſed in ſuch regular apartments, as, my guide ſaid, had acquired it the appellation of Seraija or palace. Theſe places, it is ſaid, were inhabited by banditti; and I ſaw on the way ſide near them, a large number of ſepulchral ſtones, ſtained with red, to denote that the blood of thoſe, that were there interred, was ſpilt by violence. It took us thirteen hours to Ballawadin (eighth poſt houſe) where we reſted till ſeven o'clock, Tueſday morning the 16th of May. It was here that upon our arrival, a fellow addreſſing himſelf to me as head of the party, proceeded without further ceremony to ſhampoo me. It is a cuſtom in the Turkiſh baths to preſs with both hands upon every limb and joint, and by croſſing and bending them to their utmoſt ſtretch, bring the muſcles to their proper tone: it does not produce the moſt agree-

able

able fenfations during the operation, but, after hard riding, is the compleateſt reſtorative to
ſtrength and vigor that can be imagined*.

The road from this place is acrofs a plain, for
the moſt part under water; a bridge however,
compofed of a great number of arches over the
deepeſt part of it, affords a dry paſſage to the traveller. In this part of the country grows the pop-
py, from which opium is made; fruitful and extenſive crops were ripening to the expecting pea-
fant's wiſh. Having croſſed the plain and being
arrived at the foot of the oppofite mountains, we
followed their direction, and were refreſhed and
delighted, by paſſing over at ſhort intervals, plen-
tiful torrents of water, nouriſhed by the melting
ſnow on the mountain heighths and running into
the plain.

In fix hours we arrived at Iffaklee (ninth poſt
houfe) and dined, but loſt no time. We refumed our journey with freſh horfes, and procceded
along the fame delightful plain, ſtill copiouſly
fupplied at little diſtances by torrents of refreſh-
ing water, from the fnow-top'd mountains, all the

* Vide Letter, p. 28.

X   way

way to Afkefhaher—only feven hours' ride from
the laft poft houfe and the tenth from Conftantinople.

THIS is the firft town in Caramania, fituated
at the foot and in the chafm of a mountain. It
gave birth to the famous Naffer il Din, celebrated
for his great wit and pleafantry. His fpirit is in-
voked as the genius of the place; and they report
of him, that unlefs certain unremitted attentions
are paid to him by the inhabitants, he caufes the
frefh winds to ceafe, and reduces them to defpair.
In his life time the great Zingis Khan paffed before the town, and Naffer il Din was deputed by
the inhabitants to appear before him, and to pay
their homage to him. But as the cuftom of the
Eaft makes it criminal to go into the prefence of
the Great for the firft time without fome tribute,
and the poverty of the place could offer nothing
but the fruit in feafon; old Naffer il Din had a
difpute with his wife, whether he fhould take
pomegranates or figs : fhe was for the former, but
he took the figs, in which he had good caufe to
triumph; for when he prefented the figs, the
conqueror ordered his people to throw them one
by one at his head; and for every one that hit
him, he was obferved to make a folemn thankf-
giving

giving to God. Zingis Khan could not refrain from demanding the reafon of this from the philofopher, who explained himfelf by faying, that if he had brought the pomegranates, his *wife* would have had caufe to triumph, by feeing him return with his head broken. It muft have been therefore the work of Providence that infpired him to take the figs in oppofition to her opinion; whom, for quiet fake, he had humoured in every other inftance of his life. Zingis Khan, for this witticifm endowed him with the fovereignty of the place, and which has been facred to his memory ever fince.

FROM the town we defcended again to the fame fine plain, and after ten hours ride, that is, at one o'clock in the morning, we reached Il Ghaun (eleventh poft houfe) 17th of May; three hours reft fufficed us. At four we mounted to proceed on a ftage of eighteen hours. The firft part over uneven ground, though a rich foil, to Khabung Khané, and fo on to Ladik, a town half way. It was time to reft and recruit our horfes and ourfelves for nine hours further ftretch, upon nine hours already performed with the fame horfes, was fomething redoubtable both to man and beaft. In two hours however on we went. Our road

X 2

was

was over little hills about half the way. At near sun-set we came in sight of Conia, then at a great distance, standing majesticly on an extensive plain, once the seat of empire. The eye is wearied with this view. A mountain stands singly in the center of the plain, seeming from rising vapours in the vast expanse, a shapeless cloud. As we approached, our objects disappeared. Night dropped her veil and closed the scene.

The way grew tedious as our nags grew weary, for nothing is so irksome as a jaded horse. Fatigue, and some little inconveniences from long incessant riding, made me feverish, but a few hours rest repaired all that. Temperance of living, and abstinence from wine, are necessary rules to be observed in travelling. To these I ascribe my good state of health, and the facility with which I endured the fatigues, the heats, and hardships of the journey : it was ten at night before we got to Conia. The post house (being the 12th) is without the walls of the city, not to interfere with the discipline of fortified towns, nor impede the course of public intelligence and dispatch. This city stands about half way between Constantinople and Aleppo,

and

and makes a diftance by my computation of near five hundred miles.

HAVING performed it in eight days, fome little indulgence might confcientioufly be taken; we therefore determined to fpend the night and next day, at Conia. The walls are not fo ruined as the generality of thofe city walls which have fallen under the Turkifh yoke: there are many baftions yet complete, and many monuments of the power and paffage of Sultan Amurath over this country. There are divers pieces of fculpture inferted in the walls, and particularly a coat of arms, having two fpread eagles for fupporters and another for the creft, incomparably well engraved. On the wall leading to the right from the principal gate, are two figures of lions, as big again as life, projecting from the wall, turned towards each other, and, by their attitude and expreffion, feeming eager to attack. Many indications are apparent of its having been a great and powerful city, and indeed the fituation is fuch, as with induftry and good government, to be fufceptible of the higheft attainment of grandeur and opulence.

BEFORE

BEFORE I take my leave of Conia, I muſt remark ſomething on the inſtitution of public poſt
houſes all over the Turkiſh empire. The aſto-
niſhing heaps of bones and ſkeletons of horſes
diſperſed in and about the yard of this poſt
houſe, particularly, made it occur to me as an
object worthy of enquiry.

IT being one of the principal ſprings of all
governments, and eſſential to a deſpot, to be well
informed of the fluctuations in the inferior orders of the ſtate; this public regulation the only
one which is well followed up in Turky, has
been eſtabliſhed all over the empire. In ſuch
towns on all the high roads as are at convenient
diſtances, a number of horſes are ſtationed for
the Grand Signors Tartars, or the Tartars of
any of the Baſhas; or any of the Sultans officers
of note; or any ſubject, or ſtranger who may be
furniſhed with orders to that effect from the
ſupreme Vizir, or the governors of provinces
whoſe authority your ſituation may make you
ſtand in need of. Every horſe, for every hour's
diſtance, ſtands you in ten aſpers or two pence
halfpenny; and the guide in ten aſpers for each
horſe for the whole ſtage: ſo that a ſingle traveller

veller with his guide going a ftage of ten hours
will pay for the two horfes - ~ of. 4s. 2d.
And for his guide - - 0 0 5
                                  —————
                                  0 4 7

That is four fhillings and feven pence for a ftage
of forty miles.

But as this pay is very inadequate to the charge,
it becomes the concern of the public to defray
the deficiency; and therefore, they appoint an
agent to adminifter the functions of a poft mafter; that the office may be regularly performed,
and the due proportion of each with juftice afcertained. It had been in many places, a reafon
of extortion to the Bafha's, who under pretence
of affeffing a rate for the purpofe of maintaining
a due number of men and horfes for their indif-
penfable fervice, have oftentimes fleeced the poor
inhabitants of ten times the needful. On this
account in fome places where a certain fpirit of
liberty has fhewn itfelf, the principal inhabitants
have agreed to take this duty by turns on themfelves; and in fuch places it is common to meet
with extraordinary good horfes.

At

At Conia they were mere lanthorns. The neareſt ſtation to this great city being a ride of ſixteen hours at leaſt, no horſe can poſſibly re-ſiſt it for any length of time. It follows that the mortality is very great, and the charge of courſe ſo heavy, as to make it incredible, with-out ocular demonſtration, to thoſe who are forced to ſupport it. For this reaſon the agent or Menzel Aga is cautious enough to preſerve the ſkeletons in evidence of his honeſty, and to ſcreen himſelf from puniſhment. It may ſeem ſtrange that ſo much regularity ſhould be an effect of tyranny and oppreſſion; but as thoſe who have the power to enforce it, are ſo inti-mately intereſted in its punctual adminiſtration; it is likely to continue; and to be the moſt du-rable, as it certainly is the moſt uſeful inſtitu-tion, in this tottering empire.

At five in the evening (18th May) we mount-ed and rode twelve hours along the plain to a village called Iſmil, where it was incumbent upon us to reſt. In ſix hours we reſumed our journey, which brought us by the iſolated moun-tain, in nine hours march to Kaiabunar, making a ſtage of one and twenty hours on horſeback. The ground is little cultivated in view of the

road

road, but produces numberlefs beautiful flowers, aromatic herbs, and almoft univerfally over the plain, the abfynthium or wild wormwood, emitting a fragrance which embalmed the air. In this town (13th poft houfe) is a well built mofque, and at a proper diftance in front of it, a large Khan, built, both of them, by Sultan Selim upon his return victorious, two hundred and twenty years ago from Egypt. The roofs were covered with fheet lead, fupplied from a mine in the neighbourhood of the place, but now neglected.

THIS country is renowned for its fheep and goats, and for the excellence of their fleece; their pafture is in fact like that fhort fubftantial kind which grows on the fouth end of Banftead downs. We refted here till midnight, changed horfes, and proceeded before one, by the ifland of Salt, and acrofs a large marfh under water to Khortee; a village deferted in the fummer on account of the bad air, though on the border of a fine ftream abounding with fifh. Innumerable quantities of ferpents alfo infeft this river, and come floating upon its furface, with creft erect, contemning danger. Two that came within our reach from the bridge, were victims

Y   of

of their temerity, but more perhaps of the en-
mity we had imbibed in common with mankind,
againſt this natural foe to the human race. We
were tempted by the ſituation to indulge with a
pipe, than which no luxury at ſuch a time can
be greater; and having quaffed voluptuouſly for
an hour, we remounted and purſued our way.
The remainder of this poſt was over as fine a
common land as I ever ſaw, and ſo ſimilar in fact
to ſome ſituations I had been partial to in England, as to ſtir up ſome old and painful affec-
tions of my heart. I loſt the charm of the thing
in the effects of the compariſon; and for this
time was the dupe of my recollection. In riding by a ditch, we diſcovered a large ſerpent
upon the brink of it, with a toad's head in its
mouth, and the body, though ſwelled as big as
ſhe could make it, her laſt reſource, yielding
gradually to the more powerful ſuction of its
devourer. I attempted to relieve the toad, by
firing a piſtol at the ſerpent, which flaſhed in the
pan; but Selim was more ſucceſsful with a ſtone,
for he killed the ſerpent and relieved the priſo-
ner. This was in ſight of Heraclea (14th poſt-
houſe) the approach to which is very pleaſing.
Its principal avenue is compoſed of a conſiderable plantation of trees in a ſemi-circular aſpect,
and

and beyond them on a rifing ground, appears the
town, over which a lofty mountain rears its head
involved in fnow. The more immediate entrance
to the town, is by an alleé, formed by a double
row of trees on each fide, through both of which
is turned an ample ftream. You pafs a gate of
fun-burnt brick, which with the other appearances of the town, denotes that its chief orna-
ments are the gifts of nature; fimple, but fufficient. We difmounted at about eleven o'clock
in the forenoon, and refted till four in the evening. We then purfued our journey all night,
over hills and dales to Urucifla (15th poft-houfe.)
The habitations in this village are mere huts;
there is a khan but I did not look into it. They
gave us entertainment after their way, furnifhed
us with frefh horfes, and on we continued,
over and among mountains of a great height;
having a river running at the bottom, fupplied
by frequent torrents and fources of water gufhing
from the rocks above us on both fides. In five
hours we came to a bridge, which defcribes the
limits of the Caraman and Adena Bafhaliks; and
beyond the bridge is a fource of water, for its
peculiar goodnefs and fweetnefs call'd Shukher
Poaré, the fountain of fugar. Here we were over
taken by a Boftangee and his fervant, who joined us,

Y 2   and

and regaled us with a whiff of his Nergheel or Per-
fian pipe; he had left Conftantinople the day
after us, but had not delayed on the way; in
half an hour we mounted and purfued our journey together. The mountains are adorned with
numberlefs pines fantaftically planted, affording
a moft delightful fcene. In the courfe of the
laft feven hours, the two chains of mountains
which environ the great plain of Conia, and
which my memory can trace back to the plains
of Bulla Wadin; having gradually approached
each other, and now from an eaftward direction,
turn rapidly to the fouth, and round the intermediate points of the compafs quite to fouth-
weft, and in this direction continue. We met in
this day's journey, many large caravans of Turkman families, attended like the patriarchs of
old, by all their live ftock of camels, horfes,
cows, goats and fheep: along the vallies we faw
others encamped to an incredible number. They
wander as the feafons invite, from eaft to weft,
and from north to fouth, where markets offer
for their fuperfluous ftock; in fuch directions,
and in fuch proportion, fo as to find pafture dif-
tributed by the gracious hand of Providence
for their flocks. They are well cloathed, and
the females of the chiefs are accommodated with

(tackts)

(tackts) litters. Their appearance, their wealth, their simplicity, seem each of them to bespeak inextinguishable freedom.

At eight o'clock in the evening (20th May) we arrived pretty much fatigued, at Yá Illah (16th post-house) a place composed of only three huts, but under the government of a Turkman Aga, who shews no particular respect for the Sultan's officers or commands; made independent by the security of his situation. The name of the place is an invocation to God, adapted as I suppose to the danger of the pass. I could perceive rebellion in every look, word and gesture. Our Tartar Selim, who blustered or flattered as he knew the weakness or independence of his men, was obliged at this post house to assume an air of meekness; he began in an high tone of voice, but was answered with contempt: at length he submitted to pay an exorbitant fee for his horses, and was glad to get away. It was past midnight, and in a short time we began to descend the mountain. At about half way the descent, we came to a chasm, near twenty feet wide, the mountain running abruptly up on each side to a stupendous height. On the summit to the right is an ancient tower that might well annoy the pass, but its natural

defence

defence below, feems to bid defiance to the moft powerful armies. It is in my opinion, the proper line of feparation between Syria and Caramania. The narrow pafs took up an hour in the defcent, and along a dangerous and horrid road; but affording by the light of the moon, fuch awful and romantic fcenes as might feaft the wildeft imagination. Our poft-boys were unufually concerned for the fafety of our rear, perpetually warning every body not to lag. It was a journey of ftrange delight and confternation I confefs. By day light we had paffed the defile, and were got to a pleafant fountain of water in the neighbourhood of fome inhabited lands; but ftill in the mountains, and of a very fufpicious complexion, from the objects we could difcover about us. We delayed but little, and at eight o'clock (21ft May) we were repofing again in a poor man's garden, made and cultivated for the accommodation of the traveller. It was near a large khan, originally built for the paffage of the troops, and very ufeful to the caravans in rainy feafons, but otherwife feldom frequented. From this place it requires an hour's ride to an inferior order of mountains, and among thefe, four hours more to the plain of Adena, extending to the fea. We reached this

fitua-

fituation at five o'clock in the evening, and feated ourfelves by a fmall refrefhing ftream.

It was like the landing-place to our journey's end. We could fee from thence the fea of Scanderoon, and the mountains beyond it. The city of Aleppo is diftant about two hundred and twenty miles, but we were comforted at the profpect of foon arriving at our journey's end. Selim propofed that we fhould go to Tarfus inftead of Adena, it was a nearer way he faid, if there was a certainty of finding boats, but as that fcheme would only have diminifhed our journey by land to encreafe it by fea, we thought proper to decline it. Our horfes were fo much knocked up, as to retard our arrival at Adena (17th poft-houfe) till three o'clock in the morning (22d May) the thirteenth day of our departure from Conftantinople. All the way from the foot of the mountains the foil is fine, and well cultivated; exhibiting extenfive crops of cotton and corn.

ADENA is fituated on the banks of the Cydnus and Tarfus which I have juft mentioned, is famous for being the fcene of Cleopatra's magnificence, when çited by Anthony to the plains of Cilicia.

WE

WE entered on the north fide of the town, but could diftinguifh little; it was night, but in iffuing, we paffed over a bridge of fome confideration guarded on the town-fide by a tower. During our fhort ftay at Adena, we partook of the pleafure of the hot baths, which to harraffed travellers is a real pleafure, drank plentifully of iced fhorbets, eat fome delicate apples, and fmoaked our pipes. We were vifited by two Armenians, who called themfelves agents to the Englifh gentlemen at Aleppo. The country was in great diforder they faid. Ofman Bafha, made Bafha of Adena, by the intereft of Abdi Bafha, whofe Kiaia he had been, on the point of marching with an army to affift his patron in the reduction of the rebels who had infefted the environs of Aleppo for many months. They diverted me from going by Scanderoon as I had intended, becaufe they faid no Frank was there; but they did no more than comply with the defire of Selim, who was averfe to that route. It was a fcheme they were alfo perfonally interefted in, for wifhing me to take charge of a bag of five hundred dollars to Aleppo, which I had refufed, becaufe money is a lure for thieves; they prevailed on Selim to take it, and on me to take the other road, that it might be lefs expofed.

WE

WE mounted at five o'clock in the evening for Caradaſh on the ſea coaſt to embark, and about midnight came to a horde or banditti, living in houſes compoſed of cane and mud, half under ground and half above, of the moſt thief like appearance I ever beheld. Mr. —— and myſelf were enjoined not to utter a ſyllable of Frank, and mute as mice we obeyed. We ſpread our carpets upon the top of one of theſe fellow's cells, and reſigned ourſelves to ſleep.

AT three o'clock in the morning (23d May) we were rouſed, but by our own companions, and ſet off again on our journey. We had left the river to our left a little before we came to Yá illah, to purſue its courſe between the mountains, while we made ſtrait over the tops, and met it again at Adena, after the ſouthwardmoſt chain of mountains had emancipated its reſtraints and gave it free career upon the plain. We croſſed by the bridge at Adena, and, ſaw it and its beautiful effects almoſt the whole length of the plain to the ſea. In the latter part of our journey we diſturbed great numbers of antelopes and wild boars, as they lay concealed in an extenſive ſpace of lofty rye graſs, ſerving them both for food and ſhelter. There appeared ſome

Z   ruins

ruins of villages on our way to Caradafh, a ten hours march from Adena (I will call this the 18th poft houfe).

THIS is the place of embarkation. It was feven o'clock when we arrived. Fifteen boats had juft landed a caravan of goods from the bay of Seleucia going from Aleppo to Conftantinople, and afforded us choice of embarkation. Whilft Selim bargain'd for the boat, I bathed in the fea, and obferved the fituation to be Cape Malo, forming the north cape of the gulph of Scanderoon. It affords a fmall harbour for boats, being defended by two long flat rocks to the fouthward. Clofe above the beach along fhore runs a confiderable bank of fand, through which a paffage is cut in a direct line with the center of the port, having a fquare building on an eminence fronting it, intended to give fhelter to paffengers and their effects.

NEAR this place, the Englifh fhip Greyhound was wrecked in the year 1760, and on the ftrand lay one of her guns, a melancholy memento of that misfortune. I was at Cyprus at the time, the fhip had juft before been with us; it was a fubject of grief to me then; nor can I help faying now, but my forrows are revived.

AT

AT three o'clock in the afternoon we embarked, and by the evening had traverfed the gulph
and were clofe under Cape Khanzir (hog) the
fouthwardmoft cape of the gulph of Scanderoon.
During the night we had a fmart thunder ftorm
and much rain. In the morning we paffed old
Seleucia formerly in the bay of that name, but
now of Antioch. The ruins of it feem to fpread
femicircularly round the hills above the port.
The Ries, or mafter of the boat told us, it had
been an excellent harbour, but that the Turks
had deftroyed it: I could have told him the
fame ftory with additions and variations. The
bay of Antioch has Cape Khanzir to the left or
N. E. and mount Caffius to the right or S. W.
To hit the entrance of the river (Orontes) coming from the northward, you muft fteer right
for the center of the high land of Caffius, which
courfe will bring you on the line of contact between the fea and river waters. You then run
eaftward along fhore direct for a little low building on the plain marking the entrance to the
river, into which we failed for half a mile and
landed on its banks. Our Boftangee was on fhore
firft, and being an officer on public bufinefs was
firft accommodated with horfes. He had told us
that he was upon fome commiffion to the Bafha

Z 2   of

of Damascus, and that he should go along mount Cassius (which by the bye is an almost impracticable route) to Latachia. In short he took his leave and we bestirred ourselves to follow his example.

The place is now called Sovadee (which I shall deem the 19th post house) and consists of a few cane huts. There were quantities of corn in heaps near the river as if for sale ; and upon a hill to the right appeared a town of little note. Among these mountains are various sectaries of idolaters ; some of them worshipping the devil as their supreme being, and offering as the most acceptable sacrifice to his infernal highness the blood of a cock. The river abounds in eels, which are caught and salted and carried to Cyprus, and all the circumjacent ports on the coast. The Greeks and other sectaries of the christian church make a demand for this article for their seasons of lent, and a mortification it must be in my opinion to eat them. The fishery is farmed of the Basha of Aleppo, and was in the days of my consulary dignity at Cyprus, the property of a dependant of mine. It now belongs to the Hakim Bashee (or proto medico) of the Basha.

SINCE

Since Biafs has revolted, and the high road has been made impaffable by the ravages of its ufurpers, this is become the paffage for the Tartars. The Sultan's * Khafnys too, which by an irrevocable law of the empire fhould be never ventured upon fea, is forced to feek fecurity in this dangerous deviation.

Such is the convulfed ftate of this once formidable empire. Such the neceffary effects of a tyrannical fyftem of government. Oppreffion will beget rebellion. In Caramania, and the revolted provinces, you fee the people wearing a robuft and manly afpect; they have a firm emphatic tone of voice; fpeak as if animated by a love of freedom; live a rude and natural life; poffefs its beft riches, and a fpirit to defend them! can tyranny go down with thefe? what has it produced? It is the worft of all bad policy. It oppreffes its own refources. Oppreffion begets a frefh neceffity of oppreffing. What it extorts to-day will be deficient to-morrow. The end is defeated by the means. Power muft be kept up to enforce violence and to deter refiftance. Wants increafe as the refources diminifh. Authority will know of no denial, corporal punifh-

---

* Treafures.

ment

ments are inflicted and death. Thus the impoffibility of avoiding, where there is no temper
to the evil, forces to defiance. The law of defpotifm is a felf-deftroying principle, infallible,
unavoidable. The utmoft in its power is to
protract the evil day. When the members are
lopped off which were its fupport, how is this
enormous body to ftand? It muft fall, decay,
and perifh.

So much for tyranny. We procured horfes
and at ten o'clock in the morning we mounted
for Antioch. They were fad hacks, but of evil
fometimes good (á quelqué chofe malheur eft
bon) the cruelty of Abdi Bafha had fo far expanded its terrors as to make this but a mo-
mentary inconvenience. Selim felt his authority reinvigorate under thefe aufpices, and without entreaty, difmounted the firft poor peafants
we met and took their horfes. He flogged them
for remonftrating, and that with fuch a mixture
of wanton feverity, as hurt me greatly. He
thought he pleafed me. On our way, after an
hour's ride among hills, we entered a lane hedg-
ed on each fide, and watered by a rivulet running through it. Some mulberry trees by the
road fide, made us wifhful of their fruit and in
purfuit of it we fell into the garden of a Turk.
He

He was feated by a limpid ftream, in the fhade
of a wide fpreading plantane, beguiling the time
with puerile amufements, patiently waiting for
his dinner. The peculiar hofpitality of thefe
people, made us welcome partakers of his fare,
which, exclufively of the grateful feafoning liberality is wont to add, was compofed of plenty
and variety. This is one of the agreeable cafu-
alties in the chapter of accidents which falls to
the lot of travellers. It is the happinefs of me-
diocrity. Kings are ftrangers to it. But what
of thefe Scenes ? They cannot humanize the vi-
tiated fpirit of Turkifh prerogative. Emin Aga,
our humble and pennylefs companion was feized
with the contagion here, and as if the example
of the chief was a fanction for the flave, began
to beat and bully indifcriminately.

ANTIOCH is now in view (20th poft houfe).
It is fituated at the foot of a barren rock and is
encompaffed by a wall which embraces the top of
it. The Orontes wets the fkirt of the city and
has a bridge of tolerable appearance over it leading
to a principal gate. The profpect on this fide is
hilly, but beyond it, exhibits a level champain
country, capable of the higheft degree of cultivation. We entered the city at fix in the evening (24th of May) diftrefs was depicted in every
coun-

countenance. Nothing could we hear of, but the tyrannies of Abdi Bafha, excepting indeed, the heart-heaving fighs with which fuch tales are accompanied.

HERE we refted till three o'clock in the morning (Friday 25th May). The Arabs fay, "When "you hear the ftripes, look to your own back." A fignificant proverb! And as it turned out, very appofite to the circumftance of my departure from Antioch. What I heard indeed, was the prelude to a very tragic fcene, wherein I was unfortunately to be a principal actor.

WE mounted, and our road brought us, in about an hour, to one of thofe fountains, which to the honour of the Turks be it faid, are met with where fuch conveniences have been moft wanted; near almoft all the public roads in the Turkifh empire. We difmounted, and here for the firft time on our journey, Selim prayed. As the circumftance was unufual, I remarked it at the time, and as the cataftrophe which overtook him may juftify fuch a conformity with the common opinion, that mankind feel very often a prefentiment or warning of an approaching fate, I venture to afcribe Selim's new devotion to an impreffion of this fort. We rode on from the

fountain

fountain towards the iron bridge (a bridge of
ftone over the Orontes, fo called from having
the gates cafed with iron) which took us up two
hours, debating all the way, which road we
fhould take to Aleppo; for there is one by Salkin, over the mountains, but fafe: and another
by Harim, fhorter by fix hours, and over the
plain, but dangerous. All our inclinations bi-
affed to the fhort road, and Selim though he ac-
knowledged fome danger, and left the option to
me, made fo flight of it as to determine me for
the plain. I premifed however that our arms
fhould be infpected and made ready for an encounter, but Selim then treated the notion of
danger and my propofed precaution with fuch
contempt, as to perfuade me there was no neceffity for it, and I neglected it. I thought no
more about it, but being arrived at the iron
bridge, we halted half an hour to recruit the
horfes, and I profited of the time by a nap. My
fervant Matthew could not be quite fo eafy.
During my feceffion, he had employed all the
argument he could think of and his fears could
fuggeft, to diffuade Selim from the fhorter route,
for he had heard truer reprefentations at Antioch
of the danger we had to incur, than had come
to our knowledge, or than Selim would confefs.

A 2   But

But the decree was gone forth. We croffed the
iron bridge and took the dangerous road. Selim
was penfive but would not declare his reluctance.
He rode on. I could fee his confufion, and was
ruminating with myfelf on the folly of meeting
danger without preparing at leaft, the arms we
had for our defence, when Selim rode up to me.
He had juft decided the conflict in his breaft,
and feeming to rejoice in the triumph of his reafon haftened to addrefs me. " We'll not go this
road Cogia!" Why Selim? " There are no
" villages in this harim (vile) road, we'll take
" the other." Well, do as you pleafe I faid,
and in turning from that we were in, to crofs to
the other road, we were forced to penetrate
among fome very high weed. Before we were
well got out of it, we were purfued by four
horfemen fcarcely appearing above this weed,
calling out to us to furrender or we were dead
men. We faced about and told them to keep
off. The robbers came within mufquet fhot,
ftopped, and called to us again to fubmit; but
we affected to refift. Selim drawing his fabre,
in a hectoring voice called out, your carbines,
your piftols; fire at thefe fellows. My friend
the painter, and my fervant Matthew with my
carbine, had rode off. I had only one piftol to
refort

resort to, the other had flashed at the serpent and
had not been reprimed; and with that presented
at the thieves, we received their fire. I thought
to follow up their discharge with an attack; but
they were too adroit. They disabled me by a
shot through my right arm, by which my pistol
dropped to the ground. Selim was shot through
the head dead upon the spot, and two horses
were killed. Emin Aga and myself remained on
horseback in the field; he with a solitary sabre,
and I disabled. What had we to do? Sensible
as we were of our danger if the thieves should
fire again, or attack with the sabre; we had no
alternative but to trust to our horses and if possible to get away. The thieves had not offered
to advance while we kept the field, but the moment we set off, having to pass near them in our
retreat, they bore down upon us with their sa-
bres held at arm's length in their hands. I was
foremost a few yards, and consequently nearest.
The one who had intended for me, by some im-
pression which I cannot account for, changed
his direction and turned off to Emin, met him,
and with one stroke of the sabre, cut his face
close under his eyes down to the socket of his
jaws, so that the all but sever'd part, hung by
the skin upon his breast, and in this condition .

was

was he pulled from his horse, stripped to his shirt, and left for dead upon the field. My servant Matthew was got safe back to the iron bridge when I reached it. He appeared with a most gloomy look, and when I dismounted and desired him to bind up my wound, with the cloaths and all drenched as they were in blood; he melted into tears. I forgave him for having deserted me in the action. The Kaffar or guard of the bridge, three in number, and three Delahia or cavalry soldiers of the Basha, who had seen the affair from the opposite side of the river, mounted and affected to pursue, but another party of thirty thieves appearing upon the plain, they thought it prudent to return. The baggage was carried clear away. I begged them to go in search of the poor painter who had fled the contrary way, and could not possibly have escaped being cut to pieces, if the thieves had pursued him. In half an hour they found him, and brought him half naked, with the most woeful countenance I ever beheld; he was scared and did not know that he had got among friends. Emin Aga had been brought in a moment before by the serugees, his face in the condition I have described it before, hanging down and exposing all the raw and mutilated parts of his jaw and throat. My own misfortune

appeared

appeared light, compared with such a picture of deformity. His shirt all covered with gore, a most horrid spectacle. A gangrene formed in the part and killed him after a wretched and too long existence of four days. Selim was brought to the bridge, and after a legal inquest upon his body intended chiefly to determine the orthodoxy of his faith, was buried by the high road, and a stone placed over him smeared with red. I saw in poor Selim illustrated the practice I had taken notice of in the former part of this narrative, as prevailing in similar circumstances all over Turky, but I was sincerely sorry to see it exemplified by so solemn an instance of its reality. It was time to pause a little on my own condition. I was in no dismay, though it is difficult to imagine a circumstance of more distraction to the affairs of any man, than this to mine. I had learnt the doctrine of resignation from the practice of the Turks, and with them could find solace in a patient submission to the laws of necessity. Alla-kerim, said I, God is great*. It was a question with me in that situation, whether I should go on to Aleppo, and expose myself to the danger of a mortification, by bearing two days fatigue and heat, where

* Literally merciful.

a fur-

a furgeon was to be found : or return to Antioch,
which was near, in the uncertainty of finding any
chirurgical affiftance. In this fufpenfe I was pro-
videntially overtaken by a French gentleman,
Monf. de Fonton, interpreter to the French nation at Aleppo. My fervant feeing him approach,
exclaimed with joy ; here is the French drago-
man from Scanderoon ! I took him to be fome
Greek, as fuch are ufually employed by our confuls upon the fea coaft ; and as they are apt to
affume an impertinent intereft in the national
differences ; I fet him down as unworthy of my
notice. When he came up and pretended to
commiferate with me on my misfortune. I faid
to him very indifferently ; Je vous fuis bien ob-
ligé mon ami, mais, nous fommes nous autres,
én guerre, n' eft ce pas ? meaning that I expected
little from him and to humour the fuppofed character I had given Ɓim, but I was deceived : He
was an original Frenchman, humane, well-bred,
and whofe brother I was acquainted with at Conftantinople. Vous avez tort Monfieur, faid he,
de vous imaginez comme ça. Je ferois faché que
la guerre nous rendit fauvage. Vous pouvez vous
difpofer de moi. I was compleatly chagrined at
the fentiment I had uttered, fince it happened to
be fo unfortunately applied. Je vous fais milles
excufes,

excufes, mon cher Monfieur, faid I. Je ne penfe
pas ainfi des François, veuillez bien m'en rendre
juftice. Je profiterai de votre fecours, et de vos
bontés. He perfuaded me to go on with him to
Aleppo, and without a moment's hefitation, I
put my arm in a fling and mounted. It was ten
o'clock in the morning and exceffively hot, but
I fuff-red no depreffion of fpirits nor alteration in
the pulfe. We marched four hours to the ufual
ferrying place, but the boat and people were gone
to avoid the outrages of the Bafha's people, and
we had two hours farther to proceed to find it.
We croffed the river, and in three hours more
arrived at Salkin (21ft poft-houfe) a confiderable
village on the top of a hill. We halted to pafs
the night. My friend chofe to fhave, to get rid
of fo much of his ghaftlinefs as was added by his
grifly beard, and a barber was called. But this
barber was a furgeon too, and fo well fkilled,
from great practice, in cafes of fhot wounds,
that he would not fhave the painter till he had
operated upon me. I confulted Mr. Fonton upon
the fubject, and we agreed to let him drefs the
wound. He was dextrous in cutting away the
cloaths from my arm. He then probed the
wound both ways with an iron probe as thick as
my little finger, and finding no fracture, pro-
nounced

nounced that under his care it would foon be well.
He then compofed a mixture of honey, melted
butter, (as it is prepared for Turkifh cookery) a
quantity of falt, and fome pounded onions, and
opening the wound with his probe, poured at
. leaft half a pint of it through and through. He
then bound it up, brought me a clean fhirt from
his own wardrobe, and counfelled me to be quite
reconciled to my fate. Monf. Font͏n was fo
good as to fuperintend the kitchen, his fervant
having ftaid behind; and produced an excellent
foup on which I fupped and compofed myfelf
for the night. In the morning at five o'clock,
(26th May) we refumed our journey with the
fame alacrity as ever. We continued with the
fame horfes however, along a chain of mountains
and bad roads moft part of our way by the village
of Azami to Martevan, where we paffed the night;
and the next morning in four hours march we
reached the city of Aleppo. It was upon a Sunday, the 27th day of May, and after a journey of
feventeen days inclufive from Conftantinople.

MR. Abbot the conful was at prayers with
moft of the gentlemen of the Englifh factory, in
a chapel in the confulary houfe. I begged not
to difturb him, but that Mr. Freer the furgeon
might

might be defired to ftep out to me. He made his appearance in a moment, and with his kind affiftance and care, on the 15th of July, I was again able to hold the pen for the firft time and to record the fufpended account of my journey and difafter.

I took up my refidence with Mr. Charles Smith, whofe hofpitality is univerfal; with him I calmed my forrows. My firft refolution in thefe moments of tribulation was to take fome fteps to recover my papers which were of infinite confequence to my affairs, and by Mr. Smith's advice we had recourfe to the following meafures. There is an Arab Chief named Sheik Shaaban, who is generally encamped in the neighbourhood of the robbers and is refpected by them as a prodigious conjuror and mafter of divination. The truth is, he profits of this reputation to find out by his ingenuity what appears to them, the effect of infpiration*. We in the firft place wrote him a letter accompanied with fome prefents, and hoped his good genius would patronize our caufe. Affuring him further, that in that cafe, we fhould anfwer the effects of his zeal with proper facrifices and offerings. The other mea-

---

* Turcoman Jonathan Wild.

B b

fure

sure was to send a letter to Mr. Sholl, British
marine factor, at Scanderoon, desiring him to gain
the authority of Abd-ul-Rahman Basha of Bylan
who was at this time in alliance with the thieves,
and to render me with them what good offices
were in his power. The return of the messenger
from the Arab brought me a very civil letter,
and many of my papers, but those of most consequence to me remained behind. Mr. Sholl's
applications were not attended with success. I
then sent another man with promises of greater
presents to the Arab Chief, and another to the
thieves but without effect. The man who returned from the thieves told me that they were
pursued in their retreat from committing the
robbery, and dropped many things from the
horses which they left on the way. I flattered
myself from this, that by a diligent search, the
papers might be recovered, and therefore resolved
to make another effort in person. Encouraged by
this hope, on the 7th of August I departed from
Aleppo on an expedition to the thieves.

Excursion to Ghiavur Dagh, or mountain
of infidels, the nest of the Curdine robbers.

In the opinion that the portmanteau which
contained my principal papers was fallen from
the

the horfe and that my only hope was of finding it in the plain where the grafs was grown extremely thick and high; I had to provide myfelf with fuch efficiencies as feemed moft to promife fuccefs in fuch a defperate fearch.

Koider, in the firft inftance, a conductor of caravans from Aleppo to Scanderoon, and well known to the robbers, was a neceffary attendant to efcort us to their haunts; and to prevail on them when there, to trace back the ground they had rode over in their retreat with their booty. Mr. Smith fuggefted to me to take two gypfies, who, he exclaimed, have eyes like hawks: and I thought myfelf, that, a couple of fpaniels might be ufeful to traverfe the ground before us; becaufe, in the firft place, the object if they fhould fee it by furprize would fet them a barking; or if any fcent remained in the leather, which it is fufceptible of retaining for years, the dogs might difcover it by that means, where human eye could not penetrate. To compleat our outfet, a Delattia one of the Bafha's horfe guards was thought neceffary to protect us from the foldiers, as far as it was fafe for him to proceed with us, and unfafe for us to proceed without him, the whole country being in a ftate of warfare.

With

WITH this train therefore and my fervant
Matthew I took my departure for Ghiavur Dagh
at three o'clock in the afternoon. In about
four hours we got to a village, deferted, excepting by two or three who remained there, to gather in the remaining corn; upon our approach
they concealed themfelves. We fpread our carpet here, made fome coffee, turned our horfes
into the corn that was treading out, and fmoaked
our pipes in expectation as I fuppofed of re-
fuming our journey in an hour or two. It was
moonlight, and after a reafonable time I would
have proceeded, but was oppofed. There is more
danger, my guard faid, from the peafants in the
night than from the thieves. We muft wait
till day light. At fun rife therefore we mounted and paffed by fome villages totally abandoned. At others the harveft was yet treading out,
and the inftant we were efpied by the peafants,
they retreated to their houfes, armed, and as
we came near them, kept us èn bût. We made
figns of peace to them by waving our garments
in the air, and one of them came running up to
us to know our will and pleafure. He knew
Koider, but was fufpicious of the Delattia. He
made a fignal of our neutrality to the village,
upon which they laid afide their arms and received

ceived us very kindly. I was not quite eafy under this hoftile array I confefs, and was led to enquire into the caufe of this univerfal miftruft. It was owing to the uncommon cruelty of Abdi Bafha's government. He had affembled troops from all parts to reduce the pretended revolt of Killis and Antab, two principal towns in the neighbourhood of Aleppo, and inftead of pay to thefe mercenaries, he gave them free range over the country for fuftenance and what plunder might fall to their lot in war. It was like devoting the country to general devaftation. They had laid wafte all the rich territory of Aleppo, and otherwife fo barbaroufly ufed the poor peafants, as to force them to take arms in felf defence. Every village we paffed was upon the qui vive, and altogether exhibited fuch dangerous and melancholy proofs of the effects of defpotifm as is fcarcely to be defcribed. Our Delattia only ferved to encreafe our danger. We arrived fafely however in fix hours march over craggy rocks, and in continual alarm, to the encampment of Sheik Shaaban.

He received us politely in the area of his tent, entertained us with pipes and coffee, and promifed to give us every affiftance in his power. He

is

is a venerable old man, not extenuated nor de-
preffed by his years, but fedately complacent,
talkative, and affable. He declared that he had
fent us all the papers that had been found, and
that he had permitted no further communication with the Bagdafhlees (the name of the
tribe of thieves which robbed me) becaufe Abdi Bafha had proclaimed all to be enemies of the
Sultan who fhould be found in intercourfe with
them. We ftaid till next morning in this ma-
gician's camp, which was numerous and well
ftocked. He had fome good horfes picquetted
before his tent, which he expreffed a deal of
pride in. His fon, a youth of twenty, was train-
ing to the wand effeminately dreffed, with large
gold ear-rings, and affecting a prodigious fanc-
tity and folemnity of manners. In the night we
had a little alert from fome pilfering rogues of
an inferior order of Arabs, who had crept into
the camp and ftolen fome fheep and fowls in fpite
of Oberon and all his tribe. Early in the morning we took our leave and purfued our journey
acrofs the precife fpot of our encounter, marked
with the fkeletons of our horfes which were killed. We continued on to the iron bridge, and
refted there during the heat of the day. Many
Turkman encampments were to be feen in the
neigh-

neighbourhood, and many of their people paſſed
the bridge upon their daily ſcout for melons from
the cultivated grounds. An affray happened in
our preſence, in which one of their party was
killed, and ſet them all upon the ſcout back
again, with fell revenge in their looks. I expected to ſee ſome bloody ſcene, but our route
laying a different way, for this time I was diſ-
appointed. At night we reſted in a neighbouring village, and early in the morning arranged
our party for the purſuit of the day. A dozen
peaſants with guns, ourſelves, our dogs and gyp-
ſies wandered over that part of the plain moſt
likely to reward our pains, but without effect;
the next day ended as unſuccefsfully, and reſolved me then to go among the thieves.

I HOPED that they might ſtill have concealed
the portmanteau in expectation of a better reward, and I determined to engage them to diſcover it at any price. It was my laſt hope, and
away I went the ſame evening to Antioch, paſſed the night there, and continued in the morning my route to the mountains. At ten we reached Karamut Khan, the entrance of the defile
which leads to Bylan, and guarded by an officer
of Abd-ul-Raham Baſha's, to oppoſe any hoſtile
attempt

attempt from Abdi Bafha's troops. We were
neutral people, and upon an expedition to the
thieves, the allies of Abd-ul-Rahman Bafha, and
therefore welcome. This captain of the guard
was a ftout fellow and laughed with all his heart,
at the threats of Abdi Bafha. He informed us
of the fituation of the Bagdafhlees, and in about
an hour we proceeded on our way to find them.
We were within ten minutes ride of the town of
Bylan, when a friend of Koider's met us, and
told us the thieves were in a village, half an
hour's march from the road fide. I fent him to
them to fix the time and place of an interview,
which they appointed for the next day, with an
invitation to dine. In the mean time I went
and lodged at Mr. Sholl's houfe at Bylan; and
when the hour of appointment was come, I
mounted and repaired to the rendezvous. The
fituation was among mountains, and marked by
a few detached huts in which they ufually refide:
fifteen in number were fitting round the edge
of a mat fpread upon the ground. Upon my approach they rofe to receive me, but feated themfelves again when I had taken my place. They
had every one a gun fling over his fhoulder,
and were equipped in the trophies they had won.
Some of them had my cloaths on, and others

the

the bloody spoils of poor Selim and Emin; they
were in their estimation well earned triumphs of
their victory. My first salute was, health to my
friends! Who can avert the will of fate? Peace
to you, said they; welcome, welcome. I was
then served with some water by one of the thieves
to wash my hands; and after that came dinner.
It consisted of a whole sheep roasted and stuffed
with rice and dried raisins; a large pilo besides,
and some dishes of ragou'd meats, with melons,
honey, eggs, onions, and every thing that was
palatable. I was not an utter stranger to this
kind of living, and could acquit myself in the
original use of my hands and fingers with some
dexterity. This ceremony over, water was again
brought, and then pipes and coffee. This was
the time for business, and I addressed them.
We must praise God for all things; I come not
to upbraid you; the slain are at rest, my wounds
are healed, the spoil you have divided; I come
a suitor to your favour. On my head, said one
of them, you shall be satisfied. Long may you
live! Koider has explained my wishes to you;
the papers which are missing are of great concern
to me; if you know where they are, let me have
them. They threw down some papers of real
importance to me. Thanks for these said I,

C c   have

have you no more? By the beard of Koider you
should have them! what are papers to us? you
should have all the papers in the universe for a
creish: but you may have dropt them on the plain,
they may be found. Found! the Turkmans are
encamped there by thousands; do they leave any
thing? they have burnt the weed all over the
plain. Well God be thanked; I'll say no more
about them. But let me ask you, you lead a
happy life here; of how many does your tribe
consist? Two hundred and fifty families. Abdi Basha is coming to exterminate you. Exterminate! said one of them, and burst into a fit of
laughter. Why what resistance can you make to
an whole army? Our mountain will resist him,
besides are there no more thieves do you think
than the Bagdashlees? You have the greatest
renown, what other tribes are there? Hey!
to signify innumerable, the Curdes, they are all
thieves: there are the Sleikhan, Abbagee, Ash-
kurbaglee, Chaillee, Dellibekerlee, Sareeseklee,
Kiubanlee, Cutchukallee, Ravidlee, Chakallee,
Jourlee, and Azillee, all the way from Bylan to
Persia. Some work to subdue these! You are
brave fellows; but if we meet again? fear nought,
we'll escort you to the gates of Aleppo. I took
my leave. We all mounted. They took the
road

road down to the plain, and I to Bylan, whence I inſtantly diſpatched my ſervant Matthew with letters to Mr. Smith, begging him to ſend me a Tartar with the proper muniments to take me to Conſtantinople.

BEFORE he could come five days neceſſarily elapſed, and in this time I frequently ſaw the thieves; rode about the country, got acquainted with Abd-ul-Rahman Baſha, and was witneſs during my ſtay, to the paſſage of that part of the caravan of pilgrims, called the diviſion of leſſer Aſia, on its way to Mecca. It is the moſt ſplendid of any, being generally accompanied by ſome of the Sultan's family, and compoſed otherwiſe of the principal men of the empire. Abd-ul-Rhaman Baſha poſſeſſes the ſtrait of Bylan, where this caravan was unavoidably obliged to paſs, and which as the Porte had thought fit to treat him with the epithet of Rebel, he had taken care to defend. It became neceſſary therefore to negociate for the privilege of going through this ſtrait; and that the credit of their religion, on which the Turkiſh government turns as upon a pivot, might receive no indignity, they deemed it politic to loſe no time about it. The Baſha was applied to, and he as readily conſented. Not

to

to be taken by furprize, and to have a pretext
for keeping the whole town armed while they
remained at or near the place. A public wedding was folemnized, and all the great men of
the caravan defired to affift at it. There was a
prodigious affectation of joy and merriment upon
the occafion. The pilgrims who were fuppofed
to be feafted, were furrounded by the Bafha's
troops, of courfe not very eafy in fuch a fituation ;
while the Bafha was laughing in his fleeve at the
borrowed complacency and fatisfaction they were
conftrained to put on.

THEY had pitched their camp at the foot of
the mountain, on each fide the rivulet in the
vale. Bylan is built on the flope or defcent of
a rock that hangs over the town. The fite is at
the termination of a cul de fac, formed by a
dreadful chafm in the mountain. Before you
through the aperture of the rock is the fea. To
the right and left, rocks and hills of a great
height. On the verge of the rock ftood my
dwelling, befide which ran a conftant ftream of
water thence rufhing down the precipice, and
forming a pool in the valley underneath. A
cool inceffant breeze plays round the hills; I
was charmed with the beauty of the fcene. It is
the

the retreat of thofe poor Europeans whofe lot it is to live at Scanderoon for the purpofes of trade. And a heaven it is contrafted with that hellifh focus, of fcorching heats and deadly fevers.

I LEFT Bylan on the 24th of Auguft to return to Conftantinople. My journey back varied only in the following inftances. Inftead of taking the road from Antioch to Sovadee, I came to Bylan, a ten hour's ride, partly upon the plain but chiefly among mountains. From Bylan I went to Byafs, feven hours, along the fea fide, partly on the ftrand, and partly upon the rocks. From Byafs we continued along the fea fhore nine hours to Kat Callah and from Kat Callah acrofs the plain in twelve hours to Adena. Inftead of going from Bulla Wadin to the hamlet I had digreffed to in coming; I went to Corfuff Bafha, and kept the high road all the way from Aleppo to Conftantinople. I had difmiffed my fervant Matthew as an ufelefs mobile, and had no companion but my forry decrepid Tartar. I had great reafon to lament and regret the abfence of my honeft friend Selim; but a lively fellow of a Bofnian Tartar, overtaking us upon the road beyond Conia, whip and fpur, and giving me a challenge to go on with him; I left my

poor

poor wretch to take care of himſelf, and went off full ſpeed, travelling night and day to our journey's end.

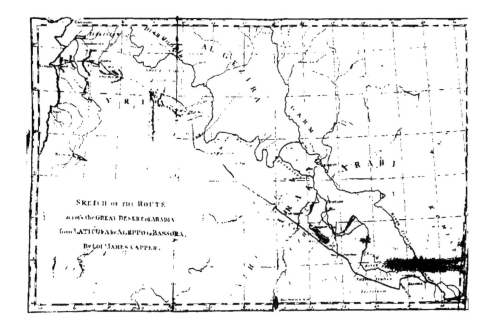

SKETCH OF THE ROUTE
across the GREAT DESERT of ARABIA
from LATICUTA by ALEPPO to BASSORA.
By Col. JAMES CAPPER.

A
JOURNAL

ACROSS THE

GREAT DESERT,

FROM

BASSORA to ALEPPO.

BY way of introduction to this journal I shall
beg leave to premise, that if Government or the
East India Company should have occasion to send
dispatches by Bassora, after the season is past for
transmitting them through Egypt; the most expeditious and least expensive manner, is by sending duplicates of the letters to our minister at
Vienna, who will forward them to the minister
at Constantinople: from thence one copy may be
transmitted to Aleppo, and another to Bagdad,
both of which in all probability will arrive at
Bassora from England, in less than two months.
The post from England to Vienna, and a courier

rier to Conſtantinople, will travel faſter and
cheaper than any gentleman; as will alſo the
Tartar couriers from thence to Aleppo and Bagdad; and when the letters contain any order or
information of more than common importance;
to enſure their ſafe arrival, a ſecond ſet of duplicates may be ſent to Vienna, and Conſtantinople, within a week after the departure of the
firſt. But ſometimes it may happen that a perſon muſt be ſent by this route, not only to convey the orders to India, but alſo to carry them
into execution; in which caſe he ſhould conſider
whether he is equal to the fatigue of travelling
all the way by land to Baſſora; if not he
ſhould go from ſome of the ports in the Mediterranean to Latichea or Alexandretta by ſea: the
former is unqueſtionably the leaſt ſubject to delays from wind and weather, but then it is alſo
by much the moſt dangerous, fatiguing, and ex-
penſive; beſides there are but few men who are
able to bear the fatigue of riding poſt from Vienna to Conſtantinople, and from thence to
Aleppo in the winter ſeaſon; and the paſſage by
ſea may be greatly ſhortened by embarking at
ſome of the ports in the S. E. part of Italy.
Upon ſumming up therefore all theſe different
reaſons, we may reaſonably conclude; that let-

ters

ters fhould be fent to Baffora all the way by land; but that a geutleman had better go part of the way to Syria by fea. Two days only were allowed me to prepare for this journey, and therefore in the midft of settling my own private concerns, I had not leifure to confider what route I had beft take; the orders given me were to go by Holland to Venice or Leghorn; in confequence of which I loft many days, which would have been faved if I had followed the abovementioned plan of going farther to the fouthward before I embarked.

It muft be entirely unneceflary to give an account of my journey to Leghorn, the way to that city being fo well known; fuffice it to fay then, that it was performed in eighteen days, notwithftanding I went round by Venice, and was detained near two days on the road; firft by the poft-mafter of Gorcum in Holland, who refufed to give us horfes to travel in the night; and afterwards by an accident happening to the carriage.

The Conful at Leghorn on our arrival there, freighted a Ragufian fnow of 220 tons to convey us to Latichea or Alexandretta, which was ready to receive us on the 27th of September 1778,

but

but the wind being foul we did not go on board until the 29th at fix in the evening. As this Journal is not intended as a direction for mariners, I fhall put down the time according to the common way of reckoning, that is from twelve at night, and not according to the aftronomical day, of twelve at noon.

On the 29th of September, 1778. At night we ftood out to fea, and got a tolerable good offing.

September 30th. The wind S. E. blowing exceedingly hard all night: in the morning we faw a fail, and likewife the ifland of Caprara, bearing about eaft, diftance feven miles, and the North end of Corfica W. S. W. The wind in the morning moderate.

October 1ft. Variable winds and calm, faw the ifland of Elba, bearing S. E. diftant about fix leagues, and the ifland of Pianofa S. by E. diftance about nine leagues, the weather cloudy; in the evening the wind veered about to the E. S. E. no obfervation.

October 2d. Variable winds and fometimes calm, faw the ifland of Monte.Chrifto, bearing E. by S. diftance feven leagues, and found a
current

current setting to the S. E. latitude observed 42. 9. N.

OCTOBER 3d. In the morning light airs, and sometimes calm: in the evening began to blow fresh from the S. W. increasing at night.

OCTOBER 4th. Continued blowing very fresh till about ten o'clock, when all at once the wind flackened, and for about an hour it became calm; and then began to blow very hard from S. S. W. we continued all night under close-reefed top-fails.

OCTOBER 5th. Light airs and calm all the day; in the night the wind freshened at S. by E. latitude observed 40. 32.

OCTOBER 6th. Calm all the morning and very hot weather; about two in the afternoon a breeze sprung up from the S. S. W. with small rain and very thick weather. In the night saw a large Moorish vessel standing to the northward, latitude observed 40. 21. N.

OCTOBER 7th. Wind at S. by E. blowing very hard all the twenty-four hours, a prodigious high sea, no observation.

OCTOBER 8th. Wind till twelve o'clock S. by E. from thence to S. S. W. blowing very

D d 2   fresh

freſh and a heavy ſea: ſaw a veſſel in the afternoon ſtanding to the N. W. latitude obſerved
40. 10. N.

OctoBER 9th. Wind from S. to S. W. a
freſh breeze and pleaſant weather, latitude obſerved 39. 40.

OctoBER 10th. Wind S. W. a freſh gale
and pleaſant weather, at day-light in the morning ſaw the iſland of Sicily, and the other iſlands
near it; Lipari, Salini, Stromboli, &c. ſtood in
ſhore till we were within about five miles of the
land, and then ſtood off and on all night, no
obſervation.

OctoBER 11th. Wind S. S. W. rather a
freſh breeze about two o'clock in the morning,
made ſail for the Pharo Meſſina, a pilot came
alongſide about ſeven in the morning, and took
the ſhip through the entrance of the Pharo,
which is about three miles broad. We paſſed
within twenty yards or leſs of the ſhore of Sicily: the price of the pilotage is not fixed, but
depends upon the weather, which being moderate, we paid only two chequins and a half; they
often demand five, and ſometimes twenty. Ever
ſince the great plague at Meſſina, there has been
a quarantine of ſeven days, even between the
coaſt

coaſt of Calabria and Meſſina; the uſual quarantine there from the Levant is at leaſt forty
days, and on the moſt trifling report of a plague,
they will not permit any body to land; in which
caſe moſt veſſels go to Malta. The center of the
channel bears about E. S. E. and W. N. W.
the wind being favourable and the weather fair,
I remained on deck the whole day to enjoy a ſuc-
ceſſion of the moſt beautiful views I ever beheld,
which would afford a variety of fine ſubjects for
our beſt landſcape painters. Off Reggio we ſaw
two French xebeques lying at anchor, but they
took no notice of us, nor of a Sicilian veſſel,
though neither of us ſhewed our colours. The
Sicilian veſſels always keep a boat a-ſtern, in
order to enable the crew to make their eſcape if
they ſhould fall in with a Barbary corſair; in
which caſe they always run the ſhip as near as
poſſible to the ſhore, and taking to the boats,
land and fly into the woods: we ſaw the top of
Mount Ætna covered with ſmoak, but it has
ceaſed emitting fire ſome years paſt. About ſix
in the evening we got through the ſtraits.

OCTOBER 12th. Wind N. W. a pleaſant
breeze and very fine weather, the ſouthermoſt
part of Sicily in ſight bearing S. W. and Cape
Spar-

Spartivento the fouthermoft point of Italy N. N. W. diftance about fourteen leagues. Saw and fpoke with a very clean Ragufian veffel homeward bound from Genoa. Latitude obferved 37. 25. N.

OCTOBER 13th. Wind S. W. by S. a light breeze and very fmooth water, with fine clear weather, latitude obferved 37. 8. N.

OCTOBER 14th. A light breeze from S. W. in the morning, which veered in the evening to S. by E. fine pleafant weather and a fmooth fea, at eight at night faw an Aurora Borealis which continued exceedingly bright for more than an hour. Latitude obferved 36. 34. N.

OCTOBER 15th. Wind from S. by W. to E. S. E. blew frefh and a confufed fea, in the night the wind came round more to the fouthward, at eleven o'clock tacked, no obfervation.

OCTOBER 16th. Wind S. W. the firft part of the day light breezes, increafing towards the evening to a moderate gale, rather hazy weather and a very heavy confufed fea, latitude obferved 36. 2. N.

OCTOBER 17th. Wind W. S. W. a frefh gale and pleafant weather for moft part of the day ;

day; about noon a little squall of rain, latitude observed 35. 19. N.

OCTOBER 18th. Wind S. W. a fine fresh breeze, and hazy weather, about five in the morning one of the sailors fell off the main yard overboard; we hoisted out the boat and saved him after he had been twenty minutes in the water. At seven in the morning we saw three French ships, at ten spoke to one of them, they were all from Smyrna and bound to Marseilles, they sent a boat on board to enquire whether war was declared between England and France, but our Captain pleaded ignorance: to avoid being known I had assumed the dress of an Italian sailor and therefore passed unnoticed with the rest. At half past five in the evening saw the land bearing N. E. distant five leagues, we imagined it to be Goza off the N. E. end of Candia.

OCTOBER 19th. Wind W. S. W. a fine breeze and very pleasant weather, saw the island of Candia, at six in the evening Cape Soliman bearing N. N. W. distant about eight leagues, latitude observed 34. 44. N.

OCTOBER 20th. Wind N. increasing gale and pleasant weather, latitude observed 34. 34. N.

OCTOBER 21ft. Wind N. N. W. very light airs and fometimes calm, latitude obferved 34. 31. N.

OCTOBER 22d. Wind N. N. W. a light breeze in the morning, all the evening calm, latitude obferved 34. 21. N.

OCTOBER 23d. Wind in the morning at N. W. at three in the afternoon at W. by N. light airs and rather increafing; in the evening, faw the ifland of Cyprus, the next morning Cape Baffa appeared bearing about N. E. diftant about twelve leagues, Cape Blanco N. by E. diftant five leagues, Cape Gatto E. by N. nine leagues. Near Baffa was fituated the ancient Paphos, of which probably Baffa is only a corruption. In the country near this Cape the women are ftill remarkably beautiful, in other parts of the Ifland they are rather plain. The Captain finding a great and unexpected fcarcity of water, determined to come to an anchor for a few hours at Lernica in order to get a fupply; latitude obferved 34. 22.

OCTOBER 24th. Wind S. W. blowing rather frefh from ten in the morning, found a current fetting W. S. W. it drove us twentyone miles in twenty-four hours, Cape Gatto N.
½ E.

¾ E. diſtant about five leagues, latitude obſerved
34. 36. At five in the evening arrived in the
road of Lernica, the landing place bearing W.
by S. and the flag of the Engliſh factory W. N.
W. diſtant off ſhore about a mile and a half.
Found lying here a French frigate from Malta;
in the evening we went on ſhore to the Ragu-
ſian Conſul's houſe, whom we enjoined ſtrict
ſecrecy, and obliged him before his ſervants to
treat us as common ſailors; we returned on board
again about eight at night. The town is built
as other common Turkiſh towns are, with bricks
dried in the ſun. After we went on ſhore, a
boat from the French frigate went on board our
veſſel, but did not diſcover any thing relating to
us. We ſaw the Engliſh Conſul on ſhore, but
he did not know us in our diſguiſe of Italian
ſailors; and we did not make ourſelves known to
him, leſt his ſervants might publiſh our arrival.

OCTOBER 25th. In the morning till about ten
o'clock calm, then a light breeze ſprang up from
the E. S. E. at eleven the captain came on board
with a Greek Pilot, and we weighed anchor with
an increaſing wind, ſaluted the French frigate
when we got under way with five guns, ſhe returned only one.

E e   Oc-

OCTOBER 26th. Wind variable moftly from the S. W. and frequently calm; in the night quite calm; at day-break faw part of the coaft of Syria; in the evening at fun-fet the mountains of Antioch diftant about fifteen leagues, latitude obferved 35. 2. N.

OCTOBER 27th. Light breeze at N. E. by N. Latichea bearing about N. E. ¼ E. about eight leagues diftant. Stood off and on all night the wind being contrary, we could not get into port, and we began to be apprehenfive that the captain of the French frigate would by fome accident hear of our being on board, and follow to make us prifoners. Saw feveral lights on the fhore in the night.

OCTOBER 28th. Light winds at N. E. La-tichea bearing N. E. by E. in the evening came on board three French boats belonging to merchant veffels then laying in the harbour to affift us in getting in. At nine at night towed by the boats, we came to an anchor in eight fathom off the entrance of the port.

OCTOBER 29th. In the morning we went on fhore to the houfe of Mr. Sciperas, Englifh Vice Conful under Mr. Abbot at Aleppo, to whom

we

we fent a letter announcing our arrival, and informing him of our bufinefs.

THE prefent city of Latichea lies about a quarter of a mile from the old port, which in its priftine ftate muft have been a moft expenfive and magnificent work, but is now in ruins; and the ground like that of the new port of Alexandria, fo foul from the blocks of marble and ftone that are fallen into it, as to deftroy the cables of fhips. The adjacent country was once famous for producing excellent wine, but there is none made now; which as the country ftill produces abundance of grapes, and the Mahomedans would not object to their being made into wine; can only be imputed to the ignorance or the indolence of the Chriftians and Jews, who together conftitute the major part of the inhabitants. The tobacco of this country is in very high efteem with the Turks and Arabians, and is now produced in fuch quantities as fupply the greateft part of the Turkifh empire; it is particularly fent to Damietta in Egypt, where it is exchanged for coffee that comes thither from Mocha, and alfo for the rice that grows in the Delta. Was this country under a good government, and were the inha-

bitants

bitants inclined to be induftrious; with the advantages they have of a fertile foil, and a fine climate, they might poffefs not only every comfort, but alfo every luxury this world produces: a remark indeed! equally applicable to almoft the whole of the Turkifh empire, which is unqueftionably the fineft part, at leaft of the old world. Where nature has been fo bounteous, it is a pity her choiceft gifts have been fo badly beftowed.

October 30th. We remained at Latichea getting our baggage on fhore, and fettling accounts with the captain. What leifure time we had both this day and the next was fpent in walking about the city, and examining the environs of it, in which there are many noble monuments of antiquity in a very ruinous ftate: towards the S. E. part of the prefent city is a large triumphal arch, fupported on columns of the Corinthian order, and which now makes part of a mofque: the architrave is adorned with antient military trophies, and there are many Greek infcriptions about the different parts of the building; but thefe have probably been much defaced by the Mahomedans. About half a mile north of the city we faw feveral fepulchral chambers, in which many ftone

coffins

coffins are depofited in fmall niches exactly made
to receive them. In the center of one of thefe
vaults is a fpring, the water of which is faid to
produce very miraculous effects; not only cur-
ing all forts of diforders, but alfo enduing people with the gift of highland fecond fight; the
Greeks call it the cavern of St. Tecla.

SATURDAY, November 1ſt. At eight o'clock
in the morning we fat out for Aleppo on horfeback, with mules to carry the baggage, and efcorted by two Janizaries; the firſt part of the
road was a ſtrong uneven country: about ten
o'clock we croffed a rivulet, and in the forenoon
began to enter the hills which are covered with
wood; the road through them is narrow, and
the afcents and defcents are ſteep, but the horfes
being fure-footed and accuſtomed to the road, we
met not with the leaft accident; the foil is a
kind of chalk, and large loofe ſtones: the har-
veſt and vintage had been over fome time, but
the peafants brought us fome grapes they were
drying for their winter ſtock. At three in the
afternoon the muleteers ſtopped near a fmall ho-
vel, where they demanded a kafar of four dollars; the diftance from Latichea I fhould fuppofe
to be about twenty-five miles. As there was
no

no houfe near we were obliged to fleep in the open air by the road fide.

NOVEMBER 2d. At two in the morning we proceeded on our journey, and ftopped about noon at the town of Chokoor, commonly called Shogre, where the governor ordered us to halt for the night. The caravanfera being dirty we paffed through the town, and lay in an open field to the S. E. of the town, on the banks of the river Orontes. On this day's journey we paffed over many chalk hills reflecting a very ftrong heat, but the road was much better than that we had paffed over the preceding day: we faw both to the right and to the left of us many confiderable towns and fome villages, the inhabitants of which brought us great variety of grapes. The town of Chokoor is fituated on the Weft fide of the river Orontes, and is furrounded by a very beautiful country. A man who called himfelf a catholic prieft, but dreffed like a Turk, and who fpoke no European language, offered us an apartment in his houfe in the town; but we preferred the field in order to get away early in the morning, before the gates would be opened. The moon fhining exceedingly bright, at midnight we began to prepare for our departure; but

but were detained by a frefh order from the Governor, who fent us word he had information of
fome Bedouins being in the road; and that in the
morning he fhould fend a guard with fome money to Aleppo, who would alfo efcort us.

NOVEMBER 3d. About four o'clock we left
Chokoor, accompanied by a large caravan, and
efcorted by horfe and foot. At fix in the morning we came to a kind of cuftom-houfe, where
they receive the kafar; at which place the people made us halt and difmount, till the whole
caravan came up to pafs the hills together. We
were told the Arabs were pofted among the hills
in the front, however we faw nothing of them;
two Turkifh horfemen exceedingly well mounted and armed, who compofed a part of our guard,
advanced in front with us to reconnoitre. We
were about an hour in paffing the hills; the road
over them was exceedingly bad, but afterwards
we went through a very fine country, where we
faw a great variety of vines, and alfo fig and olive
trees. About three o'clock we ftopped at the
town of Adelip, or Eidlip, at a fmall houfe in
the fuburbs: our comrades the Turkifh foldiers
had intereft enough in the town to get us a very
excellent pilo and fome fruit, of which without
much

much entreaty we prevailed on them to partake; we found them very fociable and ufeful companions; one of them had ferved againft the Ruffians, and gave us a very good account of the war.

NOVEMBER 4th. At two in the morning we proceeded on our journey over a very ftoney road, and kept a few hundred yards in front of the caravan, until we arrived at Khantaman; and then about nine o'clock in the morning advanced by ourfelves over a hilly and ftoney country to Aleppo. We got thither in about two hours and a half, and our baggage arrived about two hours after us. Some Arabs on bad horfes feeing us without any attendance, endeavoured to terrify us with an account of there being plunderers on the road, but no perfon attempted to moleft us; however Mr. Abbot informed us we had been imprudent in quitting our guards.

To attempt giving a defcription of a place fo well known as Aleppo would be ridiculous, efpecially as we had but little leifure for obfervation. Dr. Ruffel who refided many years in this city, has written a full and accurate account of it, which I would recommend to the perufal of every perfon who wifhes to be acquainted either with the natural hiftory of the country, or the manners and cuftoms of the inhabitants. I fhall principally confine myfelf to a detail of our own proceedings.

Upon our arrival we waited on Mr. Conful Abbot who very kindly invited us to take up our refidence in his houfe. When a ftranger comes to remain any time in the city, it is cuftomary for every European gentleman in the place to pay him a vifit, which of courfe muft be returned; but as we were only fojourners, Mr. Abbot had prevailed on them to difpenfe with this ceremony with refpect to us. He however conftantly invited company to his houfe every day, by which means we had the pleafure of feeing all the ladies and gentlemen of the place. The language moft in ufe amongft the Europeans is the Italian; however moft of them fpeak alfo the French and Englifh, and many of the ladies are converfant in modern Greek, Turkifh, and Arabic. The European languages they acquire from each other, the Greek from the women fervants, and Arabic from the inhabitants of the country and their men fervants. Even the children fpeak the major part of thefe languages with fluency and correctnefs. The Eu-

F f

ropeans by a general fubfcription have built a
fmall theatre, which they have fitted up with
great tafte. During the winter feafon they perform French and Italian comedies, and even
fometimes attempt operas with very great fuccefs;
they politely offered to exhibit fome little piece
to amufe us, but the houfe being difmantled for
the fummer, we could not ftay long enough for
them to make the neceffary preparations. We
declined accepting all invitations of either din-
ners or fuppers, but Monfieur Perdriaux, the
French conful, would not hear of a refufal, he
infifted upon our meeting a fmall private party,
which he entertained with great elegance and
good humour.

THE confuls of all nations always wear the
European drefs, but the gentlemen of the factories generally put on the Benifh or long Turkifh robe, with a hat and wig, which has an un-
couth not to fay a ridiculous appearance. Surely
it would be both more convenient and becoming,
either to confine themfelves to the European
cloaths, or elfe to adopt entirely thofe of the
Turks. The cuftom of wearing the hat in the
room with the ladies, ftrikes a ftranger alfo as
being very extraordinary; but this is done in
'com-

compliance with the opinions of the Mahomedans, who deem it indecent to appear with the
head uncovered.

As there was no caravan likely to fet out for
Baffora, the Conful was obliged to form a light
caravan exprefsly for us. He at firft agreed with
an Arabian Sheick or Chief for an efcort of forty
men to fet out in a few days, and the Sheick as
ufual was to furnifh camels for carrying ourfelves, our baggage and provifions; but a Jew
merchant hearing of our intention, offered to
double the efcort, provided we would take thirty
camels loaded with goods for him to Graine.
After fome deliberation his propofals were agreed
to, on condition that he would alfo fend two
camels for each load of goods; thefe points being fettled, a new agreement was drawn up with
the Sheick, of which the following is a literal
tranflation.

*Tranflation of a contract with the Sheick
Suliman for an efcort of Arabs acrofs
the Great Defert from Aleppo to Baffora.*

" THIS writing is to certify, that we the underwritten of the tribe of Arabs Nigadi, have

F f 2   of

of our own free will agreed to accompany and conduct the bearer of this contract, Colonel Capper, an Englishman, and those of his company: and that we oblige ourselves to take with us seventy guards of the tribes of Arabs Nigadi, and Agalli, and Benni Khaled, who are all to be armed with muskets: we the underwritten are included in the number, excepting Sheick Haggi Suliman Eben Adeyeh.—And we do promise also to carry with us nine refeeks with their muskets, two of whom of the two different tribes called Edgelefs, two of the two tribes of Il Fedaan, one of the tribe of Welled Aly, one of the tribe of Benni Waheb, one of the tribe of Lacruti, one of the tribe of Baigee, and one of the tribe of Sarhaani, making in all nine refeeks as above-mentioned.

AND it is agreed, that we the underwritten are to bring with us our own provisions for the guards and refeeks above-mentioned, and the same provisions are to be loaded upon our camels, the hire of which camels is to be paid by us; and we likewise agree to buy ourselves thirteen rotolas of gunpowder, and twenty-six rotolas of balls, the cost of all the aforesaid things are to be paid by us, and not by Colonel Capper.

AND

AND we alfo oblige ourfelves to provide for him and his people nineteen camels, for the ufe of himfelf and his company, to carry their tents and baggage, water and provifions for themfelves and for their horfes, befides thofe nineteen camels above-mentioned; we alfo oblige ourfelves to provide them two other ftrong camels to carry the mohafa, in order that they may change every day one camel, and to provide a perfon to lead the camel that carries the mohafa from Aleppo to Graine, and moreover we will appoint him a perfon to take care of his horfes.

WE the underwritten do promife Colonel Capper, by our own free will and confent, and oblige ourfelves to pay all kafars and giawayez (that is to fay duties) to all the Arabs, and to the Sheick Tamur, the Sheick Tiveini, and all the Sheicks of the tribe of Beni Khaled, and to all other tribes of Arabs whatever; and we make ourfelves refponfible for all what is above-written, and further when we approach the tribe of Arabs called Il Aflam, and Shammer and any other tribes, we oblige ourfelves to take from them a refeek to walk with us till we have paffed their confines,

WE

WE agree to carry no goods, or even letters from any other perfon or perfons, excepting the goods from Khwaja Rubens, which are thirty-one loads, for the hire of the faid goods from Khwaja Rubens we have received in full, that is, the hire, the inamalumi, the refeeks, the giawayez, figmaniah, and all other expences to Graine; we have received of him in full, according to the receipt in the hands of the faid Khwaja Rubens: moreover we have agreed with our free will to provide for the faid thirty-one loads, for every load two camels, in order to keep up with the above-mentioned Colonel Capper, and never feparate from his company till our arrival at Graine; and we alfo oblige ourfelves to pay the dolleels (fcouts) the maadeb, the birakdar, and the chaous (officers of the guards) all the faid perfons we are to pay ourfelves, and not Colonel Capper. We have agreed alfo with our free will, with the faid Colonel Capper, to carry him and his company fafe in thirty-fix days to Graine, from the day we depart from the village of Nayreb; but in cafe the faid Colonel Capper fhould be defirous of ftaying to reft a day or more the faid delay is not to be reckoned in the aforefaid thirty-fix days. And we the underwritten alfo engage three days before our arrival at Graine,

to

to difpatch a meffenger from our parts with
Colonel Capper's letter to the agent of the Bri-
tifh nation in Graine. And by this inftrument
it is ftipulated and agreed between the faid Colonel Capper and us the underwritten perfons,
that he pays us for all the fervices above-mentioned dollars nine hundred forty-one and one
fourth in Aleppo, which fum we have received
in full; befides which the faid Colonel Capper
does oblige himfelf to give us on the road dollars
five hundred; and moreover on our fafe arrival
at Graine, on our having fulfilled this our agreement with him, he the faid Colonel Capper
obliges himfelf to pay us dollars eight hundred
rumi, and in cafe we fhould fail in performing
any part of our agreement with him, we then
are to forfeit the laft-mentioned eight hundred
dollars, and all we the underwritten are refponfible one for the other, for the performance of
the promifes as above agreed between the con-
tracting parties. In witnefs whereof, we have
figned with our fingers this the fixteenth day of
the moon called Shewal, in the year of the He-
gira, one thoufand one hundred and ninety-two.

Suliman Ebben Adeyah—Mohamed il Bifhir
—Ally Ebben Faddil—Haggy Ifa Ebben Ha-
meidan

meidan—Naffeh Ebn Refheidan—Suliman Ebben Gaddib—Mohamed Ebn Nidghem—Suliman Ebben Naaifay.

The witneffes to the agreement are.

Il Haggi Omar Ulleed—Ifmael Eftracy—Il
Haggi Mahomed Firous—Il Haggi Ibrahim
Ulbed—Il Haggi Mahomed Emin il Takrity—
Il Haggi Fathu Ebn il Haggi Ufuph Maadara-
loy—Ifmael Ebben Achmed Tecrity.

IN this manner all caravans that crofs the great
defert are formed; that is to fay, an Arab Sheick
or Chief of known good charaĉter and great experience, engages a certain number of refeeks
or affociates to join with him in furnifhing the
merchants of the different cities with camels, to
tranfport their goods from one place to another;
and alfo each of the refeeks engages to bring a
certain number of armed men to enfure the fafety
of the caravan acrofs the defert. The refeeks
are taken from different tribes, in order to leffen
the rifque of being attacked; for each of them
carries the colour or enfign belonging to his tribe,
all which colours are difplayed upon the appearance of a party on the defert; and if the party
belongs to the fame tribe as any of the refeeks,

the

the principal Sheick or Chief of each tribe, having generally half of what each refeek receives from the merchants; the caravan of courfe paffes unmolefted. The firft-mentioned Sheick referves to himfelf the executive power and command in chief of the caravan; but in cafes where there is time for deliberation, a council of all the refeeks is called, and the point in debate is fettled by a majority of voices.

Many travellers give the Arabs an exceeding bad character, reprefenting them as a faithlefs and rapacious people, in whom no confidence can be repofed. I confefs they do not appear to me in that light; they certainly like moft men endeavour to make the beft bargain they can for themfelves; but for my own part, I never found them inclined to exact more than was juftly their due. My reafons for thinking favorably of them will appear in the courfe of my journal.

On the 10th of October, in the morning our baggage, fervants, and camels left Aleppo; and in the morning of the fame day we took leave of our friends, and I am fure on our parts, not without very fenfible concern at leaving fuch an agreeable fociety. We found our encampment at the village of Nayreb, about fix miles from

G g   Aleppo,

Aleppo, where the Conful had fent his fervant with a fupper; we paffed the night in an Arabian houfe as agreeably as could be expected all circumftances confidered.

On the 11th, at day-break in the morning the Conful affembled all the principal Arabs, our fervants, and in fhort all our dependants; and having given them his final inftructions with pofitive commands to treat us with the greateft refpect, he and his brother returned to Aleppo. Mr. Shaw, one of his clerks ftayed to go another ftage with us, in order that we might by his means be fupplied with any thing we might have forgotten, whilft we were in the neighbourhood of Aleppo. At feven in the morning, we marched, and in nine hours arrived at the ruined village of Haglier; at the diftance of about two miles from it we faw a falt water lake, the length of which appeared to be upwards of ten miles, to the right were fome hills not very high. About two miles from Haglier we paffed a large village of houfes, fhaped like bee-hives, near to which we met about fifty Arab horfemen, but they did not offer to moleft us: the road was good all the way, at four o'clock in the evening we encamped on a hill.

Novem-

NOVEMBER 12th. We remained at Haglier to get water and feed the camels, so that they might travel two or three days without a fresh supply. As my valet de chambre was sick, I endeavoured to prevail on him to return to Aleppo, but he being violently against it, I did not send him away; however at the same time not to be distressed for a servant I prevailed on Mr. Shaw to leave his man an Armenian who was accustomed to travelling, and who agreed to go with us for one hundred dollars and his expences paid back. Mr. Shaw left us about four o'clock in the afternoon, we had a little rain about eleven o'clock, the wind at S. W. In the evening we were joined by a small caravan going to Bagdad. Our own party to pass the desert now consisted of Major Thomson, whom I met at Aleppo in his way to India; Mr. C. Dighton who accompanied me from Europe; Jean Cadeo a Frenchman my valet de chambre; Babeck a cook hired at Aleppo; and Mr. Shaw's servant an Armenian, eighty armed Arabs, ten of which were Sheicks or Chiefs, and the rest their servants and dependants. Khawja Rubens agreeably to his promise sent sixty-two camels for thirty-one loads, and we had nineteen camels for carrying our tents, provisions and water, besides two al-

ter-

ternately to carry a mohafa. We began our firſt day's journey upon camels, to fee how we liked their motion. The walk we found difagreeable, and at firſt a great ſtrain on the loins and back, but the amble is like the fame pace of a large horſe and not unpleaſant. Cadeo being ill was put into the mohafa.

November 13th. At day break we ſtruck the tents and began to load the camels, but did not get away from the ground till eight o'clock, when all the caravan began to move: for the firſt three hours and a half the road was tolerably good; to the left we faw the S. E. end of the fame falt lake we had feen before. About feventeen miles from Haglier and two miles to the right of the road perceiving fome ruins we went to look at them, and found the ſhell or outer wall of a church built of ſtrong black granite without cement; there were four large arches that appeared to have been windows, three to the fouthward and one to the eaſtward. Near to this building were alfo the remains of a very large town; the Arabs faid it had been in ruins time immemorial, and was called Aſhuck Maſhook. At a quarter before three we ſtopped upon a riſing ground, the mountain of Diaram in fight

bearing

bearing about W. by N. diſtant about three miles. On the top of it appeared to be a ruined building, where there is ſaid to be a well of exceeding good water, and much frequented by thieves. We ſaw five Antelopes but could not approach near enough to get a ſhot at them.

NOVEMBER 14th. It rained the greateſt part of the day, little wind from S. W. at five in the morning we marched and paſſed over an uneven country, the ſoil of which is a red gravelly ſand full of holes mady by rats and ſnakes; we ſaw alſo ſeveral ſnakes ſkins. At two o'clock it began to grow cloudy and thunder to the S. W. about four o'clock in the afternoon the ſtorm broke upon us with a hard ſhower of rain, which continued ſome time, and obliged us to pitch our tents in a place where there was the appearance of a caravan of camels having been lately encamped. The uſual mode of encamping is as follows; when the caravan comes to the ground, the camels which carry the tent the proviſions and the baggage are drawn up in the centre, and thoſe with the bales of merchandize form an outer circle round them, by which means their loading makes a kind of rampart; and the camels themſelves having one of their fore legs tied up

form

form another outer circle round the goods: but when there is pasture for the camels as there was this day for the first time since we left Haglier, after being unloaded they are turned loose to browze, and before it is dark one of the drivers goes out and makes a noise somewhat like that made by our herdsmen in calling the cows; on hearing which all the camels come up to him on a full trot, and return to the camp where they are tied together to prevent their straying in the night. Our course this day was nearly E. S. E.

November 15th. It rained all night, nevertheless at six in the morning we marched, but were obliged to halt again at three in the afternoon; we passed this day over a clay and sandy soil that was very slippery, on which grew furze and long grass. We killed two snakes about seven feet long and saw a large flight of wild ducks, which came from the S. W. and flew towards the N. W. our camp was situated in a bottom surrounded with small hills; on the summit of one to the N. E. is a white building which our Arabs told us was erected by a man to the memory of his horse which died near that spot, after having saved him from falling into the hands of some Bedouins by whom he was pursued.

purſued. About four o'clock we had an alarm and our people took to their arms, the perſons ſuſpected proved to be our own ſcouts.

November 16th. The rain continued the greateſt part of laſt night, and the wind blew pretty freſh from the S. W. At ſix in the morning the wind changing to due weſt it cleared up, and at ſeven we marched. We paſſed over an hilly uneven country, the ſoil nearly the ſame as yeſterday. About nine in the morning we ſaw ſix oſtriches at the diſtance from us of about half a mile. At one o'clock found the remains of a dead body, the head entire with ſome of the hair upon it, one of the arms and both the legs gone, and no fleſh on the carcaſe; about two hundred yards further lay a blue Arab jacket, our people ſuppoſed it to be the body of a courier ſent from Bagdad with diſpatches for Aleppo, who had been ſome time miſſing. A little after two in the afternoon we halted and encamped upon a plain ſurrounded by ſmall hills. Our Sheick went to the top of the higheſt to look out for Arabs, but ſaw none; he alſo in the evening ſent two ſcouts to the next watering place, which is about fourteen miles diſtant, where we are to halt to-morrow to take in a freſh ſupply of water.

Novem-

NOVEMBER 17. We began our march at a quarter paft feven in the morning, very fine weather, fent out fcouts, and quitted the direct road to prevent falling in with an enemy. We proceeded over a very uneven conntry, the foil the fame as yefterday. About twelve o'clock we faw the remains of a very large encampment which alarmed our Sheick, and made him collect the caravan to march in clofe order; about two oclock three horfemen appeared on the top of a hill to the right of us. We drew up the men who began their war dance, throwing their mufkets over their heads and fhouting with great vociferation. As we advanced the horfemen retreated, we fhowed our colours and they difplayed theirs, on which our Sheick faid they were not irreconcileable enemies. We drew off to the right, and encamped in a ftrong poft, flanked by two marfhes, and covered in the rear by a fmall hill, on which we ftationed ten men: from this hill we could plainly perceive at the diftance of about three miles, an immenfe body of Arabs, which as they had their families and flocks with them, looked like the encampment of the Patriarchs: they firft fent out a detachment of about four hundred men towards us, but finding we were drawn up to receive them, five men only advanced

ed from their main body, feemingly with an intention to treat; on feeing which we alfo fent
five of our people to meet them. A fhort con-
férence enfued, and then both parties came to
our camp and were received with great ceremony
by our Sheick; they proved to be Bedouins under the command of Sheick Fadil, amounting
altogether including men, women and children
to near twenty thoufand. After much negociation our Sheick agreed to pay a tribute of one
chequin for every camel carrying merchandize;
but he refufed to pay any thing for thofe that
carried our tents, baggage, and provifions: thefe
terms fettled, the Bedouins promifed to fend a
refeek with us, until we were paft all danger of
being molefted by any of their detached parties.
To the fouthward of us, and about four miles
diftant we could plainly perceive the ruined city
of Tiaba, but the Sheick advifed us not to vifit
it, leaft we fhould be attacked by fome ftragglers
from the Bedouin camp. Palmira, or as the
Arabs call it Tadmor, is faid to be forty-five
miles S. of this place, over the hills.

November 18th. Sheick Suliman not having fettled with the Bagdad caravan, what portion of the Bedouins demand they fhould pay,

H h   we

we remained at the fame encampment. The
Bedouins brought fome camels to fell, for the
beft of which they afked twelve chequins : our
people purchafed one and killed it to eat ; the
flefh of the camel being efteemed a dainty, the
divifion of it occafioned many difputes among
them, nor was it without fome difficulty they
were prevented by their Sheicks from fighting
for it. One of the Bedouins who was fick, being informed we were Europeans, came to afk
our advice as phyficians ; we told him we had
no medicines with us, but would write down
his cafe, and if he would carry our prefcription
to Aleppo, the gentleman there would give him
what was proper to cure him. We accordingly
wrote the letter, and the brother of the patient
fet out with it next morning exprefs, promifing
to deliver it in two days and a half. Thefe Bedouins are almoft the only tribe of Arabs, who
live according to the primitive fimplicity of their
anceftors ; they never fleep in houfes, nor even
enter a town or city, unlefs to purchafe what
they want, or to fell what they have to difpofe
of. They acknowledge no fuperior but their
own Sheicks, nor do they like moft other tribes
pay a tribute to any of the Bafhaws belonging
to the Ottoman government. In the fummer

feafon

feafon when the wells and ponds in the defert
are almoft dry, for the convenience of feeding
and watering their camels and fheep, they always
keep near the banks of fome great river: but
after the rains they move about from one place
to another, feldom remaining on one fpot longer
than a week. They compel every perfon they
meet with to pay them a tribute; but are feldom
guilty of cruelty, unlefs they are refifted, and
any of their companions are killed; in which
cafe they are very vindictive. The year before
they fell in with us, they attacked and plundered
a caravan going from Damafcus to Bagdad; but
their victory coft them dear, which perhaps
made them more readily liften to overtures of
peace from us.

NOVEMBER 19th. We marched at half after
feven in the morning, and about a mile to the
eaftward of our camp paffed by a fpring of warm
water, which in colour, tafte, and alfo in heat,
greatly refembles that of the Briftol Wells. It
is called by the Arabs Ain ul Koum: our Sheick
told us there was once an aqueduct to convey
this water from the fountain head, to an ancient
ruined city about fourteen miles from thence,
H h 2   called

called Keffer al Ackwien, or Guffur ul Bain*,
but we faw no traces of it; foon after paffing
the well we had a good view of Tiaba, which
we faw to the fouthward at the diftance of three
miles. The ground we paffed over this day was
a tolerable good mould, and capable of producing many kinds of grain. About the diftance
mentioned by our Sheick, and rather more than
a mile to the right of the road we faw Keffer ul
Ackwien, which accompanied by our Sheick we
went to examine. The building is divided into
two fquares, and a paffage between them of
about fifty paces wide, each face of the largeft
fquare is about two hundred and fifty yards long,
and thirty feet high; there are round towers at
the diftance of forty yards from each other, the
gate is in the centre of the weft front, and a
fmall round tower on both fides of the gate. In
the interior part of the largeft fquare there is the
ruin of a building, and near to it a fubterraneous paffage that leads to a kind of a cave or cel-

* None of thefe Arabs are able to write, the pronunciation
of the names of places on the defert therefore being arbitrary and
extremely different, it is almoft impoffible to afcertain their proper denomination. Many of the ruins are by the Arabs faid to
have been built by a Keffer, which certainly implies fome of the
Cæfars, but the other name is generally too much difguifed to
be known.

lar.

lar. In the S. E. angle of the fquare was a portico of the Corinthian order entire, and the fhafts of fome other columns lying on the ground, the bafes and capitals of which we could not find. The walls are built of a kind of Bath ftone, and the fmaller fquare of the fame materials; the infide of the fmall fquare is a continuation of arches in a ruinous ftate; round the top of the walls of both the fquares is a kind of a parapet made of fmall bricks and mortar, but we could perceive no cement between the ftones of the lower wall. We were prevented taking any particular plan or view of this place by the appearance of fome ftrange Arabs. Thefe ruins and many others in fight of this place, are probably remains of towns and villages, formerly dependant on Palmira. About three o'clock we halted upon a rifing ground, the Bedouins brought fome more camels to fell, but we did not purchafe any of them. Our courfe this day was about S. E.

NOVEMBER 20th. It feems the Sheick expected to be attacked by the Arabs we faw yefterday near Keffer ul Ackwien, and for that reafon kept the centries very alert all night. At feven this morning we marched over rather a

plain

plain country, the foil a light white loom, with rank dried grafs growing on it in clumps; this day we faw a great number of hares and rabbits, of which we killed feveral; at three o'clock we halted, when the caravan came firft to the ground there were a number of antelopes in fight, which immediately fled on our appearance, and we faw no more of them*. In the evening Sheick Suliman defired a hundred and five dollars to fettle his own accounts with Sheick Fadil. Weather fair, the wind at S. S. W. courfe S. E. faw two flocks of fheep and goats, bought one fheep for feven dollars, which we killed immediately, and it proved to be very fat and good; buried without any funeral ceremony an Arab of our party who died yefterday.

NOVEMBER 21ft. We marched at feven this morning over a plain country of light clay, with a kind of fern and furze growing upon it, amongft which we fhot fome hares and rabbits. The Arabs dreffed a hare for us in the following manner. They dug a hole about two feet deep in the

* A PERSON travelling for curiofity or pleafure fhould carry with them hawks or greyhounds, and they might catch plenty of game; which would be an amufement, and at the fame time very convenient.

ground,

ground, large enough to contain the hare at full length, which they filled with furze, and then set it on fire ; after the firſt parcel of furze was confumed, they put in a fecond; and then a third, until the hole was almoſt as hot as an oven : then they put in the laſt parcel of furze, and without drawing or ſkinning the hare, they placed it on the fire until the flame was extin- guiſhed : at laſt they covered up the hare with the mould, which had been heaped upon the edge of the hole, fo as to be heated by the fire, and thus they left it until it was fufficiently ba- ked. The Arabs eat ſkin and fleſh together; but we contented ourſelves with the fleſh only, which we thought a very favory diſh. We arri- ved at our ground, where we encamped about four in the afternoon, our courſe was S. E. eaſterly.

NOVEMBER 22d. Marched at feven this morning, and in the courſe of the day paſſed two hills, but on the whole the country was toler- ably plain, we croſſed one place that had the appearance of being the bed of a river, but our people differed about its name ; the foil in ge- neral was a kind of light clay with ſtones. We ſhot ſome hares amongſt the furze. At half
after

after three came to our ground at a place called Ain ul Haroof or Juab Kunnum; we found a well in a bottom and rather deep, the water of which was muddy; weather fair and exceedingly hot, at noon the wind N. W. courfe S. E.

NOVEMBER 23d. Marched at seven this morning over an uneven country, the foil, fhrubs, &c. the fame as yefterday; about twelve o'clock we paffed the bed of a river about one hundred and twenty yards wide from the appearance of the weeds and fhrubs that grew in it, the water ran from the N. E. to the S. W. it is called Suab, and is faid to be impaffable after heavy rains. We killed fome hares, but faw not fo many as for fome preceding days; we alfo faw fome Antelopes and Oftriches but at a great diftance. In the morning cloudy to the eaftward, when the fun rofe the fky looked wild; in the middle of the day the weather was exceedingly hot and in the evening cool, wind about S. E. our courfe S. E. halted at three in the afternoon : the Arabs when the wind blows from this quarter always cover their mouths with a piece of their turbans.

NOVEMBER 24th. Marched at feven this morning over a very uneven ftoney country. At twelve halted a few minutes at the bed of a river called

called Rutgur. About one o'clock came in fight of fome hills called Manget, they bore about S. E. the country we travelled over till we halted was rather plain and the foil a light mould. Stopped at half after four, the wind N. N. E. the weather fair and the middle of the day very hot, faw a few hares, fent out three fcouts to reconnoitre the next watering place, at the diftance of three days journey, courfe S. E.

NOVEMBER 25th. Marched at feven this morning, and at noon the Bagdad caravan feparated from us to proceed to the place of its deftination, they expected to come in fight of the Euphrates the next day in the evening; we were very happy to part with them, for they doubtlefs detained us very much, but we could not get rid of them without quarrelling with the Sheick, who certainly made them pay convoy money. The foil of the country much the fame as yefterday, caught a few hares; about twelve o'clock paffed the bed of a river, halted a quarter before five in the afternoon. Whilft we kept with the Bagdad caravan, I believe we travelled only at the rate of two miles an hour, but afterwards I reckon at the rate of two miles and a half an hour. Our courfe this day was S. E. by E.

No-

NOVEMBER 26th. Laſt night was a froſt, and the air exceedingly cold, in the morning the wind W. N. W. marched at ſeven, about eight o'clock ſaw on a hill to the right of us the appearance of a ruin, but we were adviſed not to go to examine it. The country we paſſed over very much the ſame as yeſterday, caught ſome hares, halted at four o'clock on the bank of a bed of a rivulet that overflows in the rainy ſeaſon.

NOVEMBER 27th. Marched at ſeven this morning, the ſoil of the country we paſſed over was compoſed of hard ſand and flints, we ſaw ſome hills to the left of us that had the appearance of ſtone, and about three in the afternoon paſſed by a deep pit, that looked as if it had been a ſtone quarry. At five in the evening halted at Haglet ul Havran, where we found a great number of wells near the ſurface. When the camels came within half a mile of the place they began of their own accord to run as faſt as they could, which the Arabs ſaid was owing to their ſmelling the water, but I am rather inclined to believe ſome of the camels knew the place : this was the fifth day they had not drank. The appearance of a large encampment having lately

lately left this place, alarming the Sheick he talked of going the next morning towards Mefhed Aly, which he fays is feven or eight days journey from hence. In the morning the weather very cloudy, and the wind at E. but it cleared up towards the evening, and at night it was a froft, courfe E. S. E.

NOVEMBER 28th. Remained near the wells till nine o'clock in the morning that the camels might drink a fufficient quantity of water, to laft them three or four days; at half after nine began our march, we paffed over a barren country, and halted at five o'clock, about a quarter after ten o'clock in the morning, we paffed the bed of a deep rivulet, when we got over on the other fide, we were met by one of our people who had been at Cubeffa to learn news : he brought word that Baffora was certainly evacuated by the Perfians, and in the poffeffion of the Arabs; alfo that Mahomed Khulleel an Arab, but a profeffed deift who had affembled a large body of troops to attack and deftroy Mecca, had been defeated by the troops and allies of the Sherreef. The other fcout did not return with the camels, this man came on foot to us, and faid he did not know where his comrade was gone: in confe-

quenc

quence of the Baffora news, the Sheick promifed us we fhould go to Baffora inftead of Graine. About twelve o'clock the wind began to blow very ftrong from the N. W. which produced cloudy weather and fome rain; halted about half paft three o'clock in the evening, courfe E. S. E.

NOVEMBER 29th. The wind continued to blow violently and exceedingly cold; we marched at half after feven, paffed over a barren country, faw to the right of us, at a confiderable diftance a flock of fheep: when we firft perceived them they were near the fummit of a hill, which made them look large, and gave them the appearance of a party of horfe. About three o'clock we came to a country covered with furze, the fame as we had feen before; caught a few hares, ftopt at half after four o'clock in the evening: our Sheick who had intelligence of fome Arabs being on the road, fent two men to a village to gain further information about them; the man who returned on foot went again on a camel to fearch for his comrade, the wind continued blowing hard all this day from the N. W. courfe S. E.

NOVEMBER 30th. Marched at half paft feven this morning, the wind blowing at N. W. exceedingly

ceedingly cold, we paſſed over an uneven country with ſome few hills of white ſtone: the ſoil
in general a ſand, and ſome few hills of white
clay, which muſt be very ſlippery in wet weather, and conſequently dangerous to travel over
upon a camel; to the N. E. of us we ſaw a hill
that had the appearance of a ruin. One of the
ſcouts returned and brought advice that there
were ſome Arabs near the watering place where
we intended to halt the next day, we therefore
determined to go another way towards the village
of Rahaly; ſaw three eagles ſoaring in the air,
courſe S. E. by E.

December 1ſt. In the middle of laſt night
a man came and confirmed the report of our
ſcouts, he ſaid he was ſent by one of our people,
but we detained him leaſt he ſhould be employed
by an enemy: about two o'clock we turned off
due S. to avoid the above-mentioned Arabs.
In the firſt part of the day we marched over a
conſiderable ſpace of ground that is overflowed
in the rains; we afterwards met with many
different kinds of ſoil, but principally gravel.
About four in the afternoon we ſaw ſome hills
of white ſand to the eaſtward of us, near which
the Sheick ſays, there is exceeding good water,
but

but we kept to the fouthward to avoid meeting the Arabs. At noon faw a large herd of goats; this evening two men came into our camp dreff- ed in the fkins of antelopes, whofe principal bufinefs is to kill thofe animals, and to carry their fkins to the adjacent towns to fell. Halted at fix in the evening, about ten miles from Ra- haly, which we fhould have reached this night if we had not been obliged to go fo much to the fouthward; the wind weftward, the morning and the evening cool, the middle of the day ex- ceedingly hot, the weather fair.

DECEMBER 2d. Marched at feven this morn- ing, after travelling about three hours and a half over loofe fand, came in fight of two large clumps of trees; we drew up the men in good order to march to the town of Rahaly, which is fituated in the middle of a large plain, and furrounded by a vaft number of date trees: about three quarters of a mile to the N. W. of the place, are two large ponds of clear water, which are fupplied by fprings. We firft halted near thefe ponds, but the Sheick advifed us to move nearer the town. It is faid to contain five or fix thoufand inhabitants who carry on a confi- derable trade with the city of Bagdad, particularly

larly in dates. The commandant or Arab governor, upon our arrival fent us a prefent of preferved dates and bread. We faw feveral large flocks of fheep and goats, and bought a fheep for four dollars; they afked half a dollar apiece for fmall fowls, which it feems are very fcarce: the trees in the neighbourhood of the town feem to cover a fpace of near fix miles, but there is no pafture for the cattle, excepting fome fern that grows between the trees; the foil is a light fand, which perhaps is the reafon the people in general have bad eyes, for when the wind blows violently from the S. E. it raifes the fand, and is faid to affect their health as well as their eyes; the fumyel or poifonous wind that blows in July and Auguft comes from that quarter. Early in the morning about a dozen of thofe people who live by catching of antelopes came into our camp; in language as well as in features, they appear to be a very diftinct people from any Arabs I ever faw, by whom they are treated in the fame manner as we treat our gypfies.

December 3d. The Sheick being told that a large body of hoftile Arabs were on the road, fent fome people to treat with them, and defired us to remain at Rahaly, until his meffengers
                                        returned.

returned. This morning about eleven o'clock, some of those Arabs came into our camp, and two of them stayed with us as refeeks. One of our servants shot two birds somewhat like a partridge, but rather larger, the breast of the male bird is covered with black spots, and the neck entirely black; the plumage of the hen bird is exactly like that of a hen partridge; the inhabitants of the town we found to be great thieves, they attempted to take every thing they could carry away unobserved. The Sheick dispatched a man to Meshed Aly, to see if there were any other hostile Arabs in the neighbourhood of that city, and also to learn if the Persians had abandoned Bassora; by their answers we were to regulate our march; the weather fair, the morning cold, the wind all the day at N. W. in the evening the weather was remarkably fine, and the air temperate. We gave the governor's brother a present of four piastres, and a Benish or long gown: this place is remarkable for fine greyhounds, we saw several in cloathing like our race horses.

December 4th. Marched at seven this morning, the first two hours we passed over a light sand, on which grew a number of thorny

bushes

buſhes and ſome furze : about nine in the morning we ſaw a clump of trees to the left, where our people told us there was a ſmall town called Ajeb, and to the right of us was a cupola built of ſtone, ſaid to be the tomb of Sheick Huzzar; ſoon afterwards we paſſed over a place that had the appearance of a lake dried up, on the ground of which we found a great quantity of white ſalt of a bituminous taſte, it ſeemed to extend a great way to the N. E. and S. W. We were about an hour and a half in paſſing over it to the S. E. we then came on a ſand and clay intermixed with gravel; about three o'clock we ſaw another clump of trees to the left of us : about five in the evening halted in a large plain of ſand and gravel, and about four miles to the N. W. of a large ruined building, but it being late when we arrived at our ground, we poſtponed viſiting it until the next morning. The Sheick ſaid it was formerly built by the Greeks, and is called by the Arabs, Khuttar. Weather fair and wind N. W.

December 5th. Marched twenty minutes before ſeven this morning. Accompanied by the Sheick and one of the refeeks, we went to examine the ruin mentioned in laſt night's journal

K k   called

called Khuttar, it is fituated on the bank of a
bed of a river, which has been, and perhaps
ftill is very deep when the frefhes come down.
The building is a large fquare, furrounded by a
wall upwards of thirty-five feet high, and each
face of it, fomewhat more than two hundred
yards in length, built of rough ftone and mortar; within the large fquare there is a fmaller
one of about one hundred yards each face, and
parallel with the outer wall : the interior part
of the leffer fquare was divided into a number of
chambers and paffages, which being in a very
ruinous ftate, we could not form any conjecture
what they had been ; we could fee no place where
there had been wells or refervoirs of water, but
the Sheick told us that water is always found
near the furface. We faw nothing like Grecian
architecture, but our people fay it was certainly
built by the Greeks : when we were leaving
this place we were alarmed by the appearance
of fome ftrange Arabs from the N. E. they appeared as foon as we got clear of the building,
but fome of our people with the caravan who
had obferved their motions coming to join us,
the ftrange Arabs perceiving them, difappeared ;
at eleven o'clock we paffed by two fmall pools
of water, which were clear but extremely brackifh :

iſh : at half after four we halted, the country we paſſed over was ſandy, and in ſome places mixed with clay ; about half after three we ſaw a number of hillocks of ſand both to the right and to the left of us, Khuttar remained in ſight, until half an hour before we encamped. Six men on camels and ſeven on foot came and encamped near us ; it appeared they were the ſame people that we ſaw in the morning, and were well known to be thieves. In the morning the wind at eaſt and very cold, the weather fair ; diſpatched another meſſenger this evening to Moſhed Aly for intelligence.

DECEMBER 6th. Marched at a quarter before ſeven this morning, and left the people behind that encamped near us laſt night ; they mentioned to Sheick Suliman that a French gentleman going to Baſſora, had been attacked and plundered ; and although much wounded was likely to live ; they ſaid the Arabs carried him to Graine, and likewiſe that the gentleman behaved very gallantly, and killed two or three of their people himſelf. The ſoil of the country over which we paſſed till twelve o'clock was a light ſand with ſome buſhes, and a few ſmall hills to the right and left of us : a quarter be-

fore

fore twelve we arrived at a place called Hidia, where there was a pool of water, furrounded with high grafs; we filled a few fkins with the water, which was clear, but very brackifh; afterwards paffed over a country, the foil of which was mud impregnated with falt, there were banks of fand to the right and left of us. At the diftance of about twelve miles E. by N. we faw the town of Mefhed, or rather Mefgid Aly, that is the mofque or burying place of Aly, who it is well-known was the fon-in-law of Mahomed, and the favorite prophet of the Perfians. At a quarter before five we encamped near a place called Birket Rahama, wind E. S. E, weather fair. One of our fervants obferving a young camel without an owner, we fent out a man who brought it into our camp.

December 7th. Marched rather before feven, the foil over which we paffed was fand with thick bufhes, faw at the diftance of about ten miles to the N. E. the town of Mefgid Aly; we could plainly perceive feveral minarets, and a large gilt cupola; our Arabs fay the latter belongs to the Mefgid or great mofque of that city; it appeared to us with great advantage, for the fun fhone on it, and made it appear extremely brilliant:

liant: as well as we could judge of the fize of
the cupola at fo great a diftance, it cannot be lefs
than the dome of St. Paul's. About twelve
o'clock we came to a hill, on which were erected
two fmall forts, the place is called Alathe. At
the diftance of three quarters of a mile from the
Weftward fort is a fpring of water, which is conveyed to the fort by a deep ditch, and is there
raifed by means of a wheel to water a fmall garden lately made about the fort, and planted with
a great number of radifhes and onions: the largeft
fort is a fquare about ninety yards each face, at
each angle is a round tower built of mud, the
infide is a ftone building of two ftories high,
built in the Mahomedan ftile: this place was
founded by our Sheick, who propofes living here
when age and infirmities compel him to retire.
He feems to expect to lay the foundation of a
very large town here, which, as there is plenty
of water and a good foil of a light mould, for the
purpofes of agriculture and gardening; and above
all its being fituated in the high road from Mefgid Aly to Baffora, and other places near the
defert, is a very reafonable expectation. A caravan that lately paffed, which came from Graine,
and was going to Bagdad told the people in the
fort, that the Montifeek Arabs have had a great

battle

battle with the Perſians near Baſſora, in which
they cut off the whole Perſian army, and thereby repoſſeſſed themſelves of Baſſora, the wind
N. E. the weather fair, our courſe about S. E.
by S. bought a ſheep, and paid three dollars and
a half for it.

DECEMBER 8th. Marched at a quarter before
ſeven this morning over a barren ſtoney country,
killed a few hares, ſaw at the diſtance of about
ten miles N. E. of us the town of Gurgam an
ancient city rebuilding. About two in the afternoon paſſed over a hill of red gravel, and at half
after four halted in a valley where there was but
very little paſture for the camels. About eight
in the evening our centinels being poſted as uſual,
one of thoſe to the weſtward diſcovered five
horſemen who fled the inſtant he fired at them.
We doubled our guards and kept under arms for
a few hours in expectation of their attacking us
with a reinforcement. The meſſenger from
Meſhed Aly not returned, nor the people that
were miſſing from the firſt place; the wind at
E. morning cold, middle of the day exceedingly
hot, the wind in the afternoon at N. E.

DECEMBER 9th. Marched at ſeven this morning, dark and cloudy to the N. W. and the
wind

wind from that quarter: the firſt three hours, a very barren ſoil, hard ſand and large dark brown ſoft ſtones, afterwards came to a hard ſand and a great many ſhrubs; half after four halted, killed ſome hares, the weather cloudy and hazy, to the N. W. we ſaw a fire which they told us was on the banks of the Euphrates.—Major Thompſon about noon miſſed his watch, but having looked at it about ten o'clock, he ſent one of the Arabs back to ſearch for it, telling him within what diſtance it muſt have fallen; the fellow very honeſtly brought it, nor was it broken.

DECEMBER 10th. Marched at ſeven this morning, paſſed over a very barren country, ſaw to the left of us three large volumes of ſmoke from the banks of the Euphrates, which the Sheick ſaid was fifteen miles diſtance: at a quarter paſt twelve halted for half an hour near ſome wells of tolerable good water, until two o'clock the ſoil continued barren, then we got amongſt ſome hills of light ſand and broken ſtones. At four o'clock a large body of Arabs appeared to the right, who ſeemed inclined to attack us, our people immediately halted and drew up towards the enemy. Some few ſhot were fired, but a

man

man advanced waving a cloth in his hand, and
began a treaty with our Sheick who went to
meet him, which put an end to hoſtilities: our
people were of different opinions concerning
them, ſome inſiſted on their being thieves who
intended to attack us in the night; the Sheick
himſelf though he called them friends adviſed us
not to pitch our tents, and alſo to be on our guard
all night. We were encamped half a mile diſtant
from the new comers, our own camels and baggage were drawn up in as ſmall a circle as poſſible; our ſuſpected enemies were divided into
two camps, one to the weſtward and the other
to the ſouthward, wind weſterly and weather
fair.

DECEMBER 11th. The ſuppoſed thieves remained quiet all night in their camps with fires
lighted; at half after ſix we began loading our
camels, but did not move till half after ſeven:
we judged it prudent to divide our men into two
parties, one of them to march in front of the
camels, and the other to bring up the rear. The
firſt two hours the ſoil was ſand with furze, and
then a barren ſtoney country; afterwards a ſand
with furze and in ſome places large ſpots that
looked like a pond dried up in ſummer. Rather
before one in the afternoon we came to ſome
wells

wells and alfo a large pond of brackifh water; from thence proceeded over the fame fort of country and foil as before till near five; and then encamped for the night: cloudy to the N. E. and S. W. a little rain between two and three in the morning; fix of the party we faw laft night joined us on the march, and were received with great cordiality by our people.

December 12th. Marched rather before feven this morning and paffed over a light fand mixt with falt, a great quantity of furze and fome bufhes; the latter part of the day the fand lay in great heaps or ledges: halted at four o'clock in a bottom; from an afcent near the camp we faw a ruin called Couria, about five miles to the fouthward, with a glafs we could perceive it was a fquare building with round towers: the morning and evening were cool, but the middle of the day was very hot, the wind variable: the water we got yefterday brackifh and exceedingly bad. At ten o'clock at night we difpatched a letter to Mr. Latouche at Baffora, to inform him of our being on the way, and defiring him to detain any veffel that might be ready to go to Bombay; one

of

of the Arabs that joined us yesterday was selected by the sheick to carry the letter*.

DECEMBER 13th. Marched at seven this morning over a very uneven country, the soil a light and deep sand. About four miles from our last night's encampment, we saw the track of a great number of camels and asses, which our people suspected to have been the encampment of a body of thieves. We turned off immediately due E. and passed over a deep sand, and a country covered with sand and bushes; in some places the ground was covered with dried mud and sand, which by the heat of the sun was hardened so as to appear like broken tiles; there was no appearance of a road. About two o'clock we observed two people at some distance from us, and sent three of our men after them, who took one of their camels and brought it to us, but the people escaped. At four o'clock halted at a place where there were a number of springs, but not much water

---

* DID not the Arabs much to their honour consider their faith once pledged as inviolable, they would not in this manner put themselves in the power of strangers, who but an instant before were in arms against them. The man delivered the letter exactly at the time prescribed and brought an answer, for which he was paid ten dollars.

in

in the wells; this evening for the firſt time we caught a deſert rat, of which we had ſeen a great number; it is an animal that reſembles very much a ſmall rabbit both in ſhape and colour, the body is about the ſize of a ſmall mole, the tail three times the length of the body, the point of which is covered with a ſmall buſh of hair; the eyes are large, full and black, the hind legs remarkably long. Weather fair, wind S. E. and very hot; paid the Sheick one hundred and ten dollars, the laſt payment of the five hundred kept for diſburſements on the road.

DECEMBER 14th. Rained at two o'clock in the morning: marched at ſeven this morning over a plain country, a cold breeze from the S. E. and cloudy, halted at four o'clock. Courſe S. E.

DECEMBER 15th. Marched at ſeven this morning over a country of light ſand and moſtly barren; at nine in the morning ſaw a man on a camel, who told us he was a meſſenger going to the Sheick of the Montiffeeks from Sheick Sidon; he alſo informed us that Baſſora was ſtill in the hand of the Perſians. In the evening we perceived ſome men on camels to the northward, but they did not come near us; we ſuppoſed them to

be

be of the fame tribe as the man that paffed in the morning; halted at five o'clock. Weather cloudy and fome few drops of rain, wind W. N. W. and very cold, courfe S. E. by E.

DECEMBER 16th. Lightning to the N. E. marched at half after feven this morning, in a very dirty thick fog that came on about one o'clock in the morning from the N. E. feparated from the caravan belonging to Khwaja Rubens, which went to Graine, and we proceeded towards Baf-fora with only fixteen men and nineteen camels. Our Sheick gave all the water to the other party, thinking we fhould arrive in the evening at the village of Coebda; but he was miftaken in the diftance; for although we kept moving on till ten, we were obliged to pafs the night very un-comfortably for want of fomething to drink : the very great concern expreffed by the good old Sheick prevented our reproaching him for his imprudence; he offered to ride all night to fearch for water, but of courfe we did not allow him to fatigue himfelf.

DECEMBER 17th. A violent fog came on again laft night, and continued fo heavy as to foak through the tent. Early in the night before the fog came on, we faw three or four fires, appa-rently

rently at the diftance of three or four miles to
the E. N. E. the Sheick informed us they were
on the banks of the Euphrates. Marched at
day-break, and at half an hour after nine came
to the village of Coebda, which had been ruined
by the Perfians; here we got fome good water,
at leaft it appeared fo to us who had not tafted
any for more than twenty-four hours. We alfo
met at Coebda the perfon we had fent with the
letter to Baffora, who brought an anfwer from
Mr. Latouche. About one o'clock we arrived at
Zebeer, another place which had alfo been deftroyed by the Perfians. In the evening Mr.
Latouche, by a fecond meffenger informed us,
that in the morning he fhould fend us mules and
an efcort; for as hoftilities ftill continued between the Arabs and the Perfians, our efcort
could not accompany us any further: the weather cleared up a little about noon, but was not
quite clear until the evening. We pitched our
tents amongft the ruins of Zebeer, and ftationed
an advanced picquet in front towards Baffora to
guard againft being furprifed by the Perfians;
nor can this precaution be deemed unneceffary,
confidering the violent animofity that fubfifted
between the two nations, of which the following relation will fufficiently explain the caufe.

WHEN

WHEN the Perfians took Baffora, they appointed Aly Mahomed governor of it, leaving with him a garrifon of feven thoufand five hundred men. Although he was fuch a monfter, as is only to be found amidft the ruins of a country; he had art enough to conceal his difpofition, until by an affected moderation, he had thrown the inhabitants of the adjacent towns and villages off their guard. In about two months however, he broke out, beginning his exceffes in the city of Baffora itfelf. The firft victim of his luft was the daughter of an Arabian phyfician, the fame of whofe beauty having reached him, he caufed her to be brought to his houfe, where he kept her for three days, and then turned her out of doors, expofed to the infults of the mob. The father had followed his daughter to the houfe of the ravifher when fhe was torn from him, and had never quitted his door; fo that he was the firft perfon to receive her when fhe was again difmiffed. He conducted her home, intending on the way, in compliance with the cuftoms of his country to put her to death; but before he could execute his intentions, his affection for his only child prevailed over his regard to cuftom; and he determined, not only to fave her life, but alfo as much as poffible by marriage, to wipe out

the

the ftain her reputation had received. He was
rich and much refpected in the city, which added
to the beauty of the girl, enabled him to get a
hufband for her; not entirely equal to her proper
rank, and former pretenfions; but at the fame
time greatly above the vulgar. The celebration
of fuch a wedding could not fail to make a great
noife, and of courfe was foon known to the
tyrant: whilft he continued fober the news of it
feemed neither to afford him pleafure or pain;
but in the firft fit of intoxication, he fent for the
father, the hufband and the wife, and afked them
how they durft prefume to difpofe of a perfon
devoted to his pleafure? without waiting to receive their anfwer, he made one of his guards
cut off the heads of the father, and the hufband,
and then compelled the woman to bring water
to wafh their blood off the hands of the execu-
tioner; nor did he ftop here, but the fequel of
his conduct was not only too fhocking, but alfo
too indecent to be related.

NOTWITHSTANDING fuch unheard of barbarity, the major part of the inhabitants of Zebeer and Coebda were fo infatuated as to continue to live within twelve miles of him; im-
prudently relying on the faith of one who had
thus

thus publicly violated all laws; both divine and human. A few, and but very few of the moſt prudent of them had left either of theſe places, when one night in a fit of drunkenneſs, and inſtigated by avarice, Aly Mahomed marched from Baſſora with a body of troops and burnt Zebeer; at the ſame time putting to death all thoſe who attempted to eſcape from the flames: from thence he marched to Coebda, where he acted in the ſame manner, and then returned to Baſſora; exulting as much in having treacherouſly maſſacred, in cold blood, a number of defenceleſs people, as if he had obtained a glorious victory over a powerful army.

Submissive as the ſubjects of deſpotic governments generally are, even under the heavieſt oppreſſions; the inhabitants of Baſſora would certainly have revolted againſt the governor, had not the city been almoſt depopulated, both by plague and famine before it fell into the hands of the Perſians. The few wretched inhabitants who ſurvived theſe dreadful calamities, could neither reſiſt their tyrant, nor eſcape from him; their number was too ſmall to hope for ſucceſs againſt his force, and to remove from the city was impoſſible: they were therefore almoſt reduced

duced to defpair when the gallant tribe of Arabs called Montiffeeks determined to refcue them from fuch a dreadful fituation.

Sheick Tamur, the chief of this tribe having collected an army of about fifteen thoufand men, advanced with a felect party of about two thoufand horfe within fight of the walls of Baffora; the remainder he left about fifteen miles in the rear, concealed in a wadi, or water courfe, near the river Euphrates which place the Arabs deftined for the fcene of action; for befides the Euphrates to the Eaft, and the water courfe to the North, there was a deep morafs to the South. Aly Mahomed who did not want for perfonal courage, no fooner perceived his enemies near Baffora, than he marched out with five thoufand chofen troops to attack them; the Arabs retreated towards their ambufcade, and were followed by the Perfians. When the Sheick perceived the Perfians had got between the water courfe and the morafs, he fallied out of the place of his concealment; and with a part of the troops having clofed up the only opening to the Weftward, he charged them fword in hand, in which being alfo well feconded by the other detachment, which had decoyed them towards the ambufcade, they together put every man of the Perfians to

M m

death,

death, not leaving one alive to carry back the news of their defeat. By an over-fight, very difficult to be accounted for, Sheick Tamur neglected to purfue his victory, and march directly to Baffora, of which doubtlefs he would have eafily made himfelf mafter; for Aly Mahomed had left only a fmall garrifon in it, who would neither have had ftrength or fpirit enough to have made any refiftance. This account we received from one of the former inhabitants of Zebeer, whom we found employed in fearching among the ruins for what might have efcaped the hands of the Perfians, when they plundered and deftroyed the place.

In the evening we fettled accounts with the Sheick, and fo far from finding him mercenary and felfifh as thefe people are generally reprefented; he behaved to us with a politenefs and liberality that would have done honour to the moft polifhed European. It will be remembered that by our written agreement at Aleppo, I was to give him five hundred dollars on the road, and eight hundred more on our arrival at Graine: the former fum therefore I kept ready to be paid to his order; but the latter I counted and fealed up in a bag to prevent any of them being loft or miflaid.

miflaid. When this bag was brought, as I was going to open it, the Sheick ſtopped me; aſking if it had been counted and ſealed up in my pre-fence: and when I anſwered in the affirmative, with a careleſs unaffected air, beſpeaking no me-rit from the action, he threw it over his ſhoulder and ordered his ſervant to put it into his trunk. The reader will eaſily believe that this mark of his confidence gave me no ſmall ſatisfaction; it was the more ſtriking from our ſituation; for had I deceived him, he durſt not have followed me to Baffora to demand redreſs. But leſt the mention of this trait of Arabian politeneſs ſhould be imputed to vanity; I ſhall at the concluſion of this work endeavour to account for the good underſtanding ſubſiſting between us, and alſo to explain the cauſes of the diſputes which too often happen between the Europeans and the Arabs.

December 18th. At eleven o'clock the mules arrived from Baffora, eſcorted by ten ſepoys belong-ing to the factory; after taking leave of the Arabs, with mutual profeſſions of friendſhip; and a requeſt from our honeſt Sheick, that we would ſend for him to accompany us if ever we paſſed that way again, we left Zebeer.

As

As the sepoys were on foot, and moved slowly, we left them with the baggage and rode on towards Baffora. About half way we were met by Mr. Abraham and Mr. Gally, two of the company's servants, who very politely came to meet and conduct us to the Englilh factory, at which we arrived rather before three in the afternoon: the appearance of Baffora was exceedingly gloomy, having as I have before obferved been almoft depopulated by a plague, a fiege, and a famine. In the year 1772, there was fuppofed to be upwards of four hundred thoufand inhabitants in the place, and on the day of our arrival, there were certainly not more than fix thoufand, including the Perfians; the principal ftreets were like a burying ground, with fcarcely a fpace of three feet between each grave.

DECEMBER 19th. Mr. Latouche endeavoured to get a country boat to convey us to Mufcat, but he could not procure one without fending to Bunder Reeg, or Bunder Aboufhaher; called by us Bunder Bufhire.

DECEMBER 20th. The difficulty of procuring a boat was increafed by an order fent from Shiras, to detain all boats for the ufe of the troops in their march to reinforce the garrifon. This day we rode about the city, which in every part of it wore the

fame

fame gloomy appearance. The few Arabian inhabitants that remain fhewed great refpect to Mr.
Latouche as he paffed along the ftreets, on account
of his generofity and humanity towards them and
their countrymen; one hundred and fifty of whom,
after the reduction of the place he redeemed
from flavery, at his own private expence, and fent
to their relations in the country: an action that
does honour to him, and even to the country that
gave him birth.

DECEMBER 21ft. News came that the Sheick
of Julfa had taken a veffel belonging to Bombay,
and fold the crew and paffengers for flaves : this
intelligence induced the gentlemen here to advife
us to ftay for a fhip, as in country boats they thought
we rifqued falling alfo into the Sheick's hands who
might treat us in the fame manner; but we were
not at liberty to ftay, having promifed before we
left England not to wait for a fhip, if a boat could
be procured.

DECEMBER 22d. The fame difficulties ftill
continued about procuring a boat, but before the
end of the month, we were promifed what is called a doa, which is a boat of twenty or thirty tons
burthen, fewed with coir rope. The boats in which
the inhabitants crofs the Euphrates, to and from
the

the city are nothing more than large round wicker baſkets lined with leather; in which they carry not only men, but alſo horſes, and ſometimes camels.

DECEMBER 23d. Enquiring into the ſuppoſed cauſe of the plague that had almoſt depopulated this unfortunate city, I found it was in general imputed to an extraordinary inundation of the river, which left a great quantity of fiſh on the deſert, and thoſe fiſh becoming putrid, infecting the air. In riding about the environs of the city we ſaw an immenſe quantity of fiſh-bones ſtill lying on the ground. The plague generally rages with moſt violence in Turky and Egypt; in March and April, at which time the weather is extremely hot. As heat ſeems to increaſe the virulence of this diſorder; as the weather is hotter in Hindoſtan than it is in Turky; as the inhabitants alſo profeſs the ſame religion, obſerve the ſame cuſtoms, eat the ſame food, live in cities built in the ſame manner, and alſo in houſes formed of the ſame materials, it is ſurprizing that the inhabitants of India have never been afflicted with this dreadful diſorder; nor indeed can I find that it has ever been known within the Tropics, not even in Arabia Felix. So far from uſing uncommon precautions to guard againſt

the

the infection; when the plague had depopulated Baſſora, the ſhips coming from thence performed only five or ſix days quarantine on their arrival at any of the ports of India. I do not ſcruple to acknowledge that theſe hints are thrown out with a view to prevail on ſome humane and enlightened philoſopher to turn his thoughts to the inveſtigation of this matter. If the plague has never reached India, nor has even been known in the northern parts of Europe for many years paſt; might not ſome reaſon be aſſigned for its ſtill continuing to rage in the milder climates between the two extremes? Could this dreadful diſorder be driven from the face of the earth, which in my poor opinion is not impoſſible; a number of valuable lives would annually be ſaved, and the Levant would no longer be embarraſſed with the tedious forms of a long quarantine. Beſides an eaſy communication being once opened between thoſe countries and Europe; it is to be hoped the abſurd prejudices which have ſo long rendered the Chriſtians and Mahomedans hoſtile to each other, would die away; and that real philanthrophy, and univerſal urbanity, would ſucceed to ſavage perſecution, and groundleſs hatred.

DECEM-

DECEMBER 24th. At five o'clock in the afternoon, Saduc Khan entered the city, at the head of about four thousand horse. His men were stout and well-made, but they were miserably dressed and accoutred. The Prince himself is a very handsome man; as indeed are most of the Persians of distinction, being the offspring of the handsomest women of Georgia and Circassia, as well as of their own country.

DECEMBER 25th. Early this morning the master of a doa came to treat with us for his boat; at first he was very exorbitant in his demand; but at length became more reasonable, and promised to make it ready without delay. It being Christmas-day Mr. Latouche invited most of the Christian gentlemen to an entertainment at the factory: amongst which we found some of the Catholic missionaries very conversable agreeable men. Although no epicure, I cannot help remarking that the flesh of the wild hog which was one of the dishes we had for dinner, was by far the finest meat I ever tasted, which is probably owing to its feeding entirely upon dates.

DECEMBER 26, 27, and 28th. Making preparations for our voyage, the Nakhuda or Captain promised to sail before new year's day.

DECEM-

DECEMBER 29th. The Nakhuda called this morning, and faid he fhould weigh anchor the next day with the ebb, which made about two o'clock in the afternoon.

DECEMBER 30th. About two o'clock we left the factory accompanied with the gentlemen belonging to it, who during our ftay at Baffora conftantly treated us with the greateft politenefs and hofpitality: they remained a little time on board the doa and then took leave; as they went out of the boat we weighed anchor with a light breeze at N. W. and the tide in our favour: in the morning we came to an anchor again at Ahoo ul Khufeeb, where we remained to get wood, rice and dates, which are remarkable cheap and good at this place; Major Thomfon ftayed behind at Baffora.

DECEMBER 31ft. Remained at anchor until one o'clock, then weighed, the wind at N. W. at twelve o'clock the wind dying away and the tide againft us, we came to again: The river is about a mile and a quarter wide all the way from Baffora, and planted on both fides with date trees, amongft which a few towns and villages are interfperfed, which have a very pleafing effect. We faw great numbers of wild ducks, and other water-fowl on the river, but could not get within gun-fhot of

N n   them.

them. At four in the evening we weighed anchor, and paffed the mouth of a river to the Eaftward, which they faid was the boundary of the Baffora country, and the beginning of the Shaub.

JANUARY 1ft, 1779. Weighed at fix this morning with a light breeze at N. N. W. at day break we loft fight of the land, fteered till twelve o'clock, E. S. E. then afterwards E. by N. by an obfervation found ourfelves in the latitude of 29. 41. North, the weather rather cloudy; we paffed feveral boats going towards the mouth of the river.

JANUARY 2d. The wind at N. W. and the weather fair; about ten o'clock we faw the land bearing South, and about one o'clock paffed Cape Bang. On the mountains of Bang, there appeared a large fort, which our people faid was built by the Greeks, and before it was in ruins was deemed impregnable.

JANUARY 3d. In the night the wind blew exceedingly hard with a high fea; the fail having been torn by the violence of the wind we lay to, whilft they cut it up to half its former fize. At day break we made fail again, but the fail being torn a fecond time, and alfo the rudder damaged, we came to an anchor off Bunder Reeg, about three

miles

miles from the fhore. We wanted to get into that place, but we had overfhot the port; and were therefore obliged to ftand on towards Bunder Abou-fhaher, called by the Europeans Bunder Bufhir. As the wind blew frefh, and the fea ran high, for want of a fail and a rudder the boat was feveral times in danger of filling. In the afternoon the wind moderated, and at four in the evening finding ourfelves off Aboufhaher, we ftood into the road, and went on fhore to our factory, where Mr. Beaumont the refident received us with the greateft politenefs.

JANUARY 4th. The doa came into the harbour; on examining her we found that fhe not only wanted all kinds of ftores, but alfo that her rudder was entirely deftroyed; the wind blew ftrong from the fouthward.

JANUARY 5th. Finding the captain dilatory in purchafing ftores and neceffaries for the voyage, we threatened to buy them for him, and to deduct the price of them out of the balance of freight, which he was to receive at Mufcat; to avoid which he himfelf bought an anchor ftock, fome fpare rope, and two fmall fails, the wind at S. E. the weather cloudy with rain.

JANU-

JANUARY 6th. The Nakhuda continued repairing his doa, and promised to be ready in the evening; wind and weather as yesterday. I made some enquiries of a man who had been at Perfepolis, concerning the present state of the ruins of that city; he called it Tuckta Jumfhid, and said that there are only a few pillars and arches left, which are almost covered with bushes. The Grecian name of Perfepolis was totally unknown to him; he reckoned it about one hundred and twenty miles from Aboufhaher. Finding this man equally in-intelligent and communicative, I enquired of him also the present state of the modern cities, and indeed of the empire in general: he informed me that Ispahan, or as he called it Isfahan, was now almost entirely deserted; the seat of Government being transferred to Shiras, where Kerreem Khan the present Sovereign, or as he calls himself, the protector, resides. Kerreem Khan was one of the ablest Generals of the famous Nadir Shah, better known in Europe, by the name of Kouli Khan; when his master was assassinated, Kerreem Khan marched towards Perfia, and having a large body of troops devoted to him, he assumed the reins of government, which he has held ever since. A Prince coming to a throne by hereditary succession, or by election, may venture to reside in an open

city

city like Ifpahan; but an ufurper muft endeavour to fecure himfelf with fortifications: for this reafon Kerreem fixed upon Shiras, which is furrounded with a wall and a ditch, fufficiently ftrong to refift the attacks of the Perfians; and in order to render himfelf ftill more fecure, he has obliged all his principal officers to bring their women into the city, from which none of them can ever go out again without his permiffion. Could any other advantages compenfate for the want of liberty, the Perfians would have no reafon to complain of the rigour of this order; for at Shiras they certainly enjoy every pleafure that can be derived from a fine climate, and a fertile foil: they have fruits and vegetables of all kinds in abundance; and of the grapes they make a wine, the qualities of which have been celebrated by their well known Poet Hafiz, who has alfo fpoke of the ladies with fuch enthufiafm, as to fay the truth, would only become an oriental writer, but ftill there is no doubt of their being extremely beautiful: nor are the arts entirely unknown there, for at Shiras, they manufacture the fineft fword blades in the world, and adorn the handles of them with an enamel which would be admired even in London or Paris. Nothing in fhort is wanting to make Perfia a terreftrial paradife, excepting a regular government. The

Ufur-

Ufurper Kerreem is now dead, and has left a number of different competitors for the throne, but whatever fucceffor he may have will find, he has much to do to unite a kingdom which for fo many years has been in a ftate of anarchy and confufion.

The great Kouli Khan ruined Perfia : the force he collected for the invafion of Hindoftan excited in the nation in general a fpirit of enterprize and adventure; and the influx of wealth from the plunder of that country, entirely deftroyed the Spirit of induftry. In confequence of which, the cultivation of the lands has been neglected, trade abandoned, and thofe troops which were levied for conqueft, having diffipated what they acquired by plunder; have ever fince been ravaging their own native country. The fate of Perfia may ferve as a leffon to all other nations, to prefer the more flow but falutary profits of trade. Superfluous wealth occafions a kind of frenzy in a kingdom, during the paroxifms of which it feems to have acquired uncommon ftrength; but being exhaufted by unnatural exertions, it at length finks down a miferable victim to its diforder*.

Janu-

---

* It has been faid that Lord Clive propofed to pay the national debt by an expedition to China : he might in a convivial moment

JANUARY 7th. The Nakhuda promifed to have the doa ready to fail in twenty-four hours, if the wind permitted. In the evening of this day there was a violent fquall of wind from the S. E. accompanied with thunder, lightning and rain, which was the breaking up of the weather; for in the night the wind came round to the northward with a moderate breeze.

JANUARY 8th. The Nakhuda called in the morning to inform us he fhould fail in the evening about five o'clock, at which time we embarked and failed in company with two trankeys bound to Gombroon, the wind N. N. W. and the weather fair.

JANUARY 9th. Fair weather with a frefh breeze at N. W. faw the mountain and Cape Burdiftan, and at twelve o'clock bore away N. N. E. towards a fhoal called the Cock, that we paffed at one o'clock in the afternoon, and upon which two Englifh fhips have been loft; one of them in the

ment amongft his friend have faid fuch a fcheme was practicable, and fo it certainly is; but he was too found a politician, to wifh to fee one hundred and fifty millions of fpecie the amount of the national debt in his time, introduced at once into England, knowing as he muft that the fudden introduction of one half of that fum, has irrecoverably ruined Perfia one of the moft highly gifted countries in the world.

year

year 1763. On the mountain of Burdiſtan they uſed formerly by ſignals of fire in the night and of ſmoak in the day to convey intelligence to the merchants at Shiras, of the appearance of the ſhips expected from India; that they might inſtantly come to Abouſhaher to purchaſe their goods. Latitude obſerved 27. 53. North.

JANUARY 10th. About two o'clock in the morning it grew calm, and continued ſo all day: about ſix in the evening a light breeze ſprung up from S. S. E. About four miles from the ſhore ſaw Cape Naband E. by N. latitude 27. 11. North.

JANUARY 11th. Calm till about ſeven in the morning, then a light breeze ſprung up from the N. W. ſaw a ſmall boat coming from the Southward, and two others from the Eaſtward, ſaid to belong to a pirate called Abd ul Rheman, they did not come within gun ſhot of us, but hovered about us till dark and then appeared no more. Within about ſix miles of the ſhore on which are high rocks called Dar ul Aſban that appeared white like chalk, latitude obſerved 27. 8. North.

JANUARY 12th. A freſh breeze from the N. W. and fair weather, paſſed by the Iſland of

Sheick

Sheick Shaub, Shudwan and Handeraby, latitude obſerved 26. 43. North.

JANUARY 13th. Calm the greateſt part of the night and this morning, at eleven o'clock came on a freſh breeze from the N. W. which continued till ſeven in the evening, paſſed by the Iſlands about five, ſaw the highland about Gombroon bearing E. N. E. latitude obſerved 26. 23. North.

JANUARY 14th. Light airs and variable, paſſed the Iſlands of Keſh and Belior, latitude 26. 24. North.

JANUARY 15th. The wind at N. E. and blew freſh, coming further to the eaſtward. In the morning we ran in towards the Iſland of Kiſmis, near a place called Daag ul Kumuck, came to an anchor after ten o'clock, calm, latitude obſerved 26. 36. North. Two people who came in a ſmall boat from the ſhore, confirmed to us the report that Mahomed Raſhid Sheick of Julfa, had taken one of the company's veſſels, going from Bombay to Baſſora, and ſold the crew for ſlaves.

JANUARY 16th. At nine in the morning weighed anchor, and went round the Weſt end of the Iſland of Kiſmis, called by the Perſians Touly, and came to an anchor again off Ras, (cape) Baſſido

O o   which

which by an obfervation lays in the latitude of 26.
41. North. The people faid that between twenty and
thirty years ago, there had been a fettlement of Europeans here; we faw the remains of a church, and
the ruins of a large town that had been built with
bricks dried in the fun. At two in the afternoon
weighed with a light breeze at S. W. and the tide
in our favor, the channel between Kifmis and the
main at this place is about four miles wide. At
Baffido we got a frefh fupply of water, which was
taken out of a refervoir that had been built by the
Europeans, paved all through with a white ftone:
at this time there were not ten houfes inhabited in
this large ruined town, all which were Perfians.

JANUARY 17th. Came to an anchor at half
paft ten at night, and did not weigh again until fix
the next morning. About feven we arrived amongft
a parcel of Iflands covered with trees moft of which
ftood two feet or more in the water; the Iflands
are divided by very narrow channels, fo that the
trees almoft meet and form a kind of arbour. About
eleven o'clock it being calm and the tide making
againft us we again came to an anchor; the people
whilft they were cutting wood faw three large
wild hogs and fome pigs. At half after eleven in
the forenoon it began to rain hard, and to blow
frefh from the N. W. which continued till two
o'clock;

o'clock; then cleared up and being a fettled wind we weighed. Until five in the evening we continued failing through a narrow channel, amongft the Iflands, and then came in fight of a fort and ruined town called Left; it is fituated under a hill on the Ifland of Kifmis; the fort bore about S. W. of us at fun fet; near this place we were obliged to wait for our boat that Sheick Aly the Nakhuda had fent on fhore for fome wood and fifh for his own private ufe. About four in the afternoon made fail again and paffed by a galivat belonging to Sheick Mahomed Miny of Ormus. No obfervation on account of the hazinefs of the weather.

JANUARY 18th. At night calm, the tide making againft us, came to an anchor. In the morning at day break weighed with a light breeze to the S. W. Gombroon bearing about N. N. E. In the afternoon the wind frefhened and came further to the weftward, blowing very hard from five to feven in the afternoon, and then it began to moderate, no obfervation. Cape Salamet on the Ifland of Mahomed Salamet bore at fun fet, about S. W.

JANUARY 19th. The wind continued to blow exceedingly hard from the weftward, which made the veffel both roll and pitch very much: at half after eight the fail was broken by the violence of the

wind;

wind; unbent it, and bent a smaller. The middle of the night being exceedingly cloudy, the Arabs for want of a compass did not know which way to steer; they had been going above two hours due North when we discovered it, and put them right; they had been deceived by a change of wind and bad steerage. In the morning came on a fresh breeze to the N. W. which continued till ten in the morning, it then grew calm, and afterwards sprung up from the same quarter: latitude observed 26. 29. North, distant from the shore about five leagues, high mountain near Cape Mozandan. The town of Lema bore of us at noon S. W. by W. the afternoon little wind and cloudy all round.

JANUARY 20th. About one o'clock this morning came on a fresh breeze at North, which increased with a following sea: about four o'clock in the morning our tiller rope broke, and it was with much difficulty we prevented the vessel from flying to. Three men got overboard to mend the rudder, in the mean time the vessel rolled so much that there was danger of her filling, or at least of her carrying away the mast; in about an hour the rudder being repaired, we got under sail again, the weather being dark and squally; the Nakhuda or Captain, and the Malleem, or pilot, thought it unsafe to continue any longer at sea, and therefore put in at Khorfa-kan,

kan, which is situated on the coast of Arabia, in a small bay open only to the Eastward; on the S. E. side of the bay is a harbour for boats, where we lay in smooth water, and entirely sheltered from all winds, it rained exceedingly hard the whole day, and consequently wetted our baggage and beds. At seven in the evening the clouds dispersed, and it began to clear up.

JANUARY 21st. About two o'clock this morning came on a very hard squall of wind and rain, with violent thunder and lightning from the N. W. which continued near an hour; had we been at sea we must inevitably have foundered in less than five minutes, for although we lay in a place surrounded with hills, the violence of the wind shook the vessel as if she had been struck by a broadside from a large ship. The wind being at S. E. we could not move, therefore at day-break we went on shore to the top of the hills to take a view of the country, and dry our cloaths, &c. on a small hill to the Westward of this little harbour, is a ruined castle, formerly built by Nadir Shah, to cover a magazine for his stores, when his troops besieged Muskat. The town which is situated at the bottom of the Bay was once considerable, but at present con-

sists

fifts only of two or three houfes built of ftone, the reft are fifhermens huts.

JANUARY 22d. At nine at night the wind being fet in at N. W. and the weather fair, we weighed anchor from Khorfakan. When out at fea we faw fome lightning from the S. E. At eleven at night the wind began to frefhen from the N. W. and at one blew in hard fqualls; at feven in the morning our tiller rope broke, which had not been mended above a quarter of an hour when a hard fquall came, and the rudder itfelf was broken: as it was impoffible to mend it without unhanging it, fome of the people went overboard for that purpofe, and in half an hour brought the remainder of the rudder on board; but it was full four hours before it was repaired: in the mean time, as we could not lay the veffel to, we lowered down the fail, and the veffel lay with her broadfide to the wind; we expected fhe would fill every moment, for the wind blew very hard in fqualls, with a fhort and heavy fea, when the rudder was mended, fix of our people got into the fea to fix it. About twelve o'clock, with much difficulty we got her head round and fcudded before the wind; juft after we had repaired the rudder, we faw Cape Shenes, bearing

weft,

weſt, latitude obſerved 24. 34. N. We had no
obſervation at Khorfakan, but from its bearing
and diſtance this day at noon; I ſhould ſuppoſe
it lays in latitude 25. 13. North.

JANUARY 23d. At ten laſt night, in ſhift-
ing the ſail to haul in for the land, our tiller-rope
broke again, and the veſſel flew up in the wind.
We tried when the rope was mended to bring
her head round again to our proper courſe, but
in vain, and therefore ſteered as much as we
could to the weſtward. Our people were ſo
much harraſſed by the fatigues of the preceding
day and night, that they could not be prevailed
upon to exert themſelves; but on the contrary
were ſulky and quarrelſome, upbraiding us with
being the authors of their diſtreſſes, in obliging
them to leave Khorfakan before the weather was
ſettled. Our veſſel being very lively ſhipped no
ſea, although the wind and ſea encreaſed conſi-
derably. At day-break in the morning, paſſed
between the iſlands of Sawady, and the town of
Sohar on the Main: the wind being much more
moderate, at five in the morning we came to an
anchor at Muſcat. The entrance of the outer
port where we anchored is defended by ſeveral
batteries even with the water's edge; but the
Arabs

Arabs with fome reafon depend moft upon two forts, erected upon hills, commanding the mouth of the inner harbour, which are called Marany and Jillaly; not being acquainted with the rules of this place, we narrowly efcaped getting into a fcrape; for as no boats are allowed to go on fhore after fun-fet from the outer port, the guards ftationed in the two above-mentioned forts fired at us; but fortunately they were bad markfmen, only one of their fhot ftruck the boat. The Succefs, Grab, from Bombay, which was bound to Baffora with difpatches, was lying in the inner harbour; we went to the houfe of Narraindofs, the Englifh broker, which although not a very elegant habitation appeared to us, who had been expofed to violent wind and inceffant rain for eight and forty hours, a perfect palace.

JANUARY 24th. In the morning Captain Twyfs came and told us he fhould fail for Baffora the next day. He had fix Englifh gentlemen paffengers with him that were going over the defert, and alfo Monfieur Borel de Bourg, the French officer, who had been plundered and wounded by the Arabs on the defert. Monfieur Borel wifhing to hear the lateft news from Europe, and perhaps alfo being defirous of con-

ver-

verfing with a perfon who had lately travelled the fame route as himfelf, came and fpent the evening with me at the broker's houfe. I told him that I was no ftranger to what had be-fallen him on the defert, and eafily prevailed on him to give me an account of his adventures.

. The particulars of the bufinefs upon which he was fent, he of courfe concealed, but in ge-neral terms he informed me that foon after the engagement between the two fleets near Breft, in July 1778 ; Monfieur de Sartine, his friend and patron ordered him to carry difpatches over land to India. I think he faid he left Marfeilles on the third of Auguft; but that owing to the ftupidity of the Captain of his. veffel, and to contrary winds, he did not arrive at Latichea be-fore the end of the month ; from thence he im-mediately proceeded to Aleppo. The French Conful could not collect more than twenty-five guards to attend him acrofs the defert; with which, on the fourteenth of September, he be-gan his journey. He met with no ferious mo-leftation, until he was within fifteen days of Baffora, when early one morning he perceived himfelf followed by a party of about thirty Arabs mounted on camels, who foon overtook him.

P p

As

As they approached, he by his interpreter defired they would pleafe to advance, or halt, or move to the right or left of him, for he chofe to travel by himfelf; they anfwered that they fhould not interfere with him, and went forwards at a brifk rate. Mr. Borel's people then fufpected them of fome hoftile defign, and told him to be upon his guard. In the evening, between four and five o'clock, he obferved them halted and drawn up as if to oppofe him; and in a few minutes three other parties, confifting alfo of about thirty each appeared in fight, in oppofite directions, feemingly inclined to furround him: from thefe appearances very naturally concluding their intentions to be hoftile, and confequently his fituation defperate, like a gallant man he thought only of felling his life as dearly as poffible; he was armed with a double barrelled fuzee, a pair of piftols, and a fabre. As he kept marching on, he firft fell in with the party in front, who fired at him, which he returned as foon as he came within mufket fhot of them, and killed the Sheick; when he had difcharged his fire arms, before he could load them again, feveral of the Arabs broke in from different fides, and cut him down. Stunned with the violence of the blow, he knew nothing

that

that paſſed afterwards, until about an hour before day-break the next morning, when he found
himſelf entirely naked on the ground, a quantity
of blood near him, and part of the fleſh of the
ſide of his head hanging upon his cheek.　In a
few minutes he recollected what had paſſed, but
as he could feel no fracture or contuſion in the
ſkull, he began to think his wounds were not
mortal: this however was only a tranſient gleam
of hope, for it immediately occurred to him,
that without clothes or even food, he was likely
to ſuffer a much more painful death.　The firſt
objects that ſtruck him when he began to look
about him were thoſe who had been killed on
both ſides in the action; but at the diſtance of
a few hundred yards, he ſoon afterwards perceived a great number of Arabs ſeated round a
large fire: theſe he naturally ſuppoſed were his
enemies; nevertheleſs he determined to go to
them, in hopes, either to prevail on them to
ſave his life, or elſe to provoke them to put an
immediate end to his miſeries.　Whilſt he was
thinking in what manner without the aſſiſtance
of language he ſhould be able to excite their
compaſſion, and to ſoften their reſentment againſt
him for the death of their companions, which
theſe people he had heard ſeldom forgive: it oc-

P p 2　　　　　curred

curred to him, that they paid great respect to age; and also that they seldom destroy those who supplicate mercy; from whence he concluded, that if he could throw himself under the protection of the oldest person amongst them, he might probably be saved. In order to approach them unperceived, he crept towards them upon his hands and knees; and when arrived within a few paces of their circle, having singled out one who had the most venerable appearance, he rushed forwards and springing over the head of one of the circle, he threw himself into the arms of him, whom he had selected for a protector. The whole party were at first extremely astonished, not having the least notion of his being alive; but when their surprize subsided, a debate arose whether or not they should allow him to live. One of them who had probably lost a friend or relation, drew his sword in a great rage, and was going to put him to death, but his protector interposed, stood up with great zeal in his defence, and would not suffer him to be injured; in consequence of which, his adversary immediately mounted his camel, and with a few followers went away. When this contest was over the Sheick, for so he happened to be, perceiving Monsieur Borel entirely without
clothes,

clothes, prefented him with his abba or outer cloak, invited him to approach the fire, and gave him coffee and a pipe, which an Arab when he is not on the march, has always prepared. The people finding Monfieur Borel did not underftand Arabic enquired for his interpreter, who was found afleep and flightly wounded.

The firft demand the Arabs made was for his money and jewels, which they obferved Europeans always have in great abundance, but which are concealed in private drawers, that none excepting themfelves can difcover. He affured them thefe opinions were erroneous with refpect to him, for that he was not a rich merchant, but only a young foldier of fortune, employed to carry orders from his government in Europe to their fettlements in India: but that if they would convey him to Graine, a place near Baffora on the fea coaft; on their arrival there, and on the receipt of his papers, he would engage to pay them two hundred chequins, about one hundred pounds fterling. After a few minutes confultation with each other they acceded to his propofals, returned him his oldeft Arabian drefs, and during the reft of his journey treated him with tolerable kindnefs and attention.

AFTER

AFTER Mr. Borel's arrival at Graine, he eafily prevailed on an Armenian to advance him the money to fulfil his engagements with the Arabs; and alfo to fend the French refident at Baffora an account of what had befallen him on the defert, defiring to be fupplied with money and other neceffaries to enable him to proceed to Pondicherry. His letter very fortunately for us fell into the hands of the Englifh refident at Baffora, who having heard of our rupture with France, was convinced he muft be charged with public difpatches of confequence, and therefore determined to arreft him. Every generous mind will lament the neceffity there was of adding to the diftreffes of this fpirited and unfortunate youth; but the lives of thoufands, and perhaps the fafety of our fettlements in India, depended upon his being intercepted; but to prevent his being treated with any rigour, or fuffering any indignity, Mr. Abraham the fecond in council of the factory, was employed to feize him.

THE town of Graine which is fituated about 70 miles S. E. of Baffora, is governed by an Arab Sheick who is very much attached to us; but Mr. Abraham knew it would be very difficult to prevail on him to violate the rights of hofpitality to a ftranger, and without the Sheick's connivance, the execution of the project would have been ab-

folutely

folutely impracticable : the better to conceal his
defign, Mr. Abraham went down to Graine at
night in a country boat, accompanied by the Captain of one of our fhips then lying at Baffora, and
immeditately proceeded to the Sheick's houfe, to
whom he communicated his bufinefs. The Arab
at firft violently oppofed the meafure; but being
mollified by prefents, and alfo affured that Mr.
Borel fhould not receive any perfonal injury, he at
laft acquiefced. When Mr. Abraham knocked at
the door, Mr. Borel was retired to reft, but he inftantly got up to admit him, thinking he was a
perfon fent from the French refident with an anfwer to his letter. As foon as he difcovered his
miftake he attempted to defend himfelf, but he
was inftantly overpowered and conveyed to the fea
fide, where he was put on board the fhip that had
been fent from Baffora, and was juft then come to
an anchor off the place. He had two pacquets,
one for Pondicherry, and another for Mauritius,
which were found ; but Monfieur Borel obferved
to me, that they miffed the key of the cypher in
which the difpatches were written, by neglecting
to fearch the lining of his cloaths. It was perhaps
a fortunate circumftance for Monfieur Borel that
he was taken prifoner by us, for his wound through
unfkilful management, and the want of proper re-
medies

medies was grown extremely bad; nor is it improbable that if he had attempted to proceed in a country boat, the only conveyance that he could have got at Graine; his wound would have occafioned his death long before the boat could have arrived at any French fettlements in India. I made ufe of thefe arguments to confole him for his misfortunes, but zeal for his country, the natural enthufiafm of his difpofition, and the hopes which had been given him of promotion, had he executed his commiffion, made him deaf to every thing I could fay to confole him. Difappointed but not difcouraged by his former fufferings, he was then on his way to Baffora to proceed over the great defert a fecond time; which I was afterwards informed, he paffed with every affiftance he could receive from the gentlemen of our factory.

JANUARY 26th. Remained at Mufcat, the wind blowing directly into the mouth of the harbour.

JANUARY 26th. Went on board the dingy at day-light, and began warping out. At eleven in the forenoon got out of the harbour and failed. The wind began to frefhen in the afternoon, and there being appearances of its blowing ftill harder, at three in the afternoon, we put about and returned into
the

the harbour of Mufcat, came to an anchor off
the fort of Merany. At feven in the evening another dingy that had failed at the fame time put back
in a very fhattered condition. The Grab that failed in the morning went away before the wind to
Baffora.

JANUARY 27th. The wind continued to blow
exceedingly hard all laft night from the S. E. Although we lay with two anchors under the cover of
a hill in fmooth water, we drove very much in the
night. At day-break layed a grappling to the weftward, and warped towards the harbour. At eight
in the morning the wind came round to the weftward, and blew very hard, with great clouds of
duft that came off the land; the veffels that were
going out, and alfo all the fifhing boats immediately put back into the harbour; as our people
feemed apprehenfive of a hard gale; by their advice
we alfo returned into the inner harbour, where we
found three dingies waiting for a fettled wind, to
proceed to the Malabar coaft with us; remained in
the harbour, as the fort would not let us pafs out
in the evening.

JANUARY 28th. At day-break in the morning
began to warp out of the harbour, and at eleven o'clock
got under fail, but firft went on board an Englifh fnow

Q q   bound

bound to Aboulhaer, commanded by Captain Johnſon who gave us a quadrant, mine having been injured by a fall; he alſo kindly offered us every other aſſiſtance in his power. The wind at N. W. at ſun-ſet Cape Curiat bearing S. W. by S. diſtant about five leagues. In the evening the wind began to ſlacken very much.

JANUARY 29th. Calm all night. Came on a light breeze this morning which laſted from ſeven to ten; calm all the reſt of the day and the weather very hazy. Latitude obſerved, 23. 15. North.

JANUARY 30th. Calm the greateſt part of the night. At four in the morning came on a light breeze to the N. W. At day-light ſaw a large veſſel to the S. S. E. ſtanding to the weſtward. Latitude obſerved 23. 9. N. Calm ſince noon, and a ſwell from the N. W.

JANUARY 31ſt. Very little wind all night. At three in the morning a light breeze ſprung up to the Southward; in the afternoon it came round to the Weſtward, and at laſt ſettled in the N. W. Latitude obſerved 22. 24.

FEBRUARY 1ſt. Light wind all day from the N. W. and very fine weather. Latitude obſerved 22. 15.

FE-

FEBRUARY 2d. Calm part of laſt night, afterwards a breeze from the N. W. continued till five in the morning. Calm till twelve o'clock. Latitude obſerved 21. 52. North. At two in the afternoon a breeze ſprung up, which continued to freſhen.

FEBRUARY 3d. Laſt night at eleven o'clock the wind came to N. E. and freſhened to a very fine breeze. At two in the morning paſſed by two ſmall dingies, ſuppoſed to be bound to Muſcat, but did not hail them. Latitude 21. 19.

FEBRUARY 4th. A freſh breeze from the N. W. and fair weather. At nine ſaw a veſſel to the N. E. quarter, ſtanding to the Southward; we hauled our wind as ſoon as ſhe appeared in ſight, ſuppoſing her to be an enemy. She paſſed within a quarter of a mile to leeward of us, without taking any other notice, but hoiſting her colours, which were Moors. Latitude obſerved 20. 30. North.

FEBRUARY 5th. Light winds at N. N. E. Latitude obſerved 19. 50. North.

FEBRUARY 6th. A fine freſh breeze at N. E. and very fair weather. At three in the afternoon layed to and ſounded, found forty-ſix fathoms; ſaw

ſevera

several snakes, the signs of being near the Malabar coast. Latitude observed 19. 22.

FEBRUARY 7th. Most part of the day very little wind, and sometimes calm. About two o'clock in the afternoon the sea wind sprung up and freshened to a fine breeze; hove to and sounded, found forty-three fathoms: latitude observed 19. 15. Course E. ¼ N.

FEBRUARY 8th. A fine fresh breeze at N. W. for the most part of the day. Saw the land at day light in the morning, and at four in the afternoon came to an anchor in Bombay harbour, found there the Asia man of war, Capt. Vandeput; the Royal Admiral and Morse Indiamen, and several other country ships. The Asia and the two Indiamen arrived from England the day before us. At six in the evening went on shore to the governor's house and delivered him the pacquets.

Mr. Hornby the governor of Bombay, during our stay on that Island, entertained us very politely at his house, and ordered a vessel to be got ready to convey us to Anjengo. On the 14th of February we embarked on board the Terrible bomb-ketch, Capt. Baine, and arrived at Anjengo in nine days; a voyage at this season of the year on

the

the Malabar coaſt is always agreeable, but was
rendered particularly ſo to us, from the good humour, and good ſenſe of our captain.

HAVING hired a palanquin and proper people
to carry it, on the 24th in the evening I ſet out
from Anjengo for Pallomcotta, and arrived there
in three days, the diſtance is ninety one Engliſh
miles.

				Miles.
From Anjengo to Bringon		—		21
Colachie	—	—	—	20
Cotata	—	—	—	15
The gate or barrier between the dominions of				
the King of Travancore and the nabob of Arcot				7
Pannagoodie	—	—	—	5
Naganachara	—	—	—	8
Pallamcotta	—	—	—	15
			Total	91

MY friend Captain Burrington, the commandant of that garriſon, detained me one day whilſt
he ſent orders to have palanquin bearers ready for
me, at all the different ſtages on the road to Madras. After leaving Palamcotta, the firſt day I
reached Madura, diſtant about ninety-ſix miles.
The ſecond day arrived at Tritchonoply ninety two
miles:

miles: here I halted half a day having reafon to believe the palanquin bearers were not ftationed. The third day in the afternoon left Tritchonoply and arrived at Cuddalore in the evening of the fourth, one hundred and eight miles: remained here a few hours, and then proceeded through Pondicherry to Madras, one hundred and fourteen miles, where I arrived in the afternoon of the fixth day. The whole diftance is eftimated at four hundred and fourteen miles, which was performed in five days and a quarter, exclufive of ftopping and a few unavoidable delays on the road. The travelling pace in a palanquin is on an average about four miles an hour.

It has been invariably my rule throughout this journal to acknowledge the attention I met with on the way; but without proceeding in the fame manner after my arrival at Pallamcotta, and from thence to Madras; I fhall only in general obferve that travellers in India are always received with a liberal hofpitality unknown in any other country. Not that I affect to fay there is more urbanity in India, than in Europe; but as moft of the Europeans in that country are known to each other; and there are no houfes of public entertainment excepting at the prefidencies; it of courfe becomes a matter of reciprocal convenience, that the chiefs at the different

ent

ent out fettlements, and the commandants of the
fortified towns fhould keep a kind of open houfe,
for all perfons who are generally known, or properly introduced to them. How kindly and hand-
fomely ftrangers are received on their firft arrival
in India is a fact of public notoriety, and general
admiration. The letters of introduction which
perfons carry out from England, not only procure them temporary civilities, but alfo obtain for
the ladies in particular fuch a reception as almoft
furpaffes belief. From the inftant of their arrival,
they are confidered as belonging to the family to
which they have been introduced, and from which
they are never again feparated, but by death or
marriage.

It is hardly neceffary to obferve, that more attention has been paid to the matter, than to the
ftile of this journal, particularly in that part of it
which relates to the defert. But the obfervations
were put down on the evening of the day on which
they were made, and with no other view than to
ferve as memoranda; in which form perhaps they
may be moft acceptable to the generality of readers,
as being the ideas of the country, as they occurred
on the fpot. It may be thought that too much
has been faid of wind and weather, which are feldom much noticed in books of travels by land.
When

When travelling in a clofe carriage, it certainly
does not fignify what quarter the wind comes from,
or whether it blows hot or cold: but this is not the
cafe with a traveller expofed to the open air, with
no other covering than the cloaths he wears. A
perfon going acrofs the defert will probably be glad
to know what weather he is likely to meet with
on his journey, that he may equip himfelf properly; and neither be encumbered with any thing
fuperfluous, nor neglect taking any thing really
neceffary.

A PARTICULAR confideration of the character
of the Arabs and a more minute defcription of the
defert than is contained in this journal are kept as
materials for a larger work. Neverthelefs for the
convenience of travellers who in the mean time
may pafs that way, and for whofe ufe this journal
was originally publifhed; it may be proper to give
a general idea of the defert and its inhabitants, by
means of which the traveller will readily become
acquainted with the principal difficulties he has to
encounter; and alfo with the difpofitions of the
perfons with whom he is about to affociate.

THE great Defert of Arabia has often been reprefented as an immenfe fpace of barren fand, which
never has nor ever can be made to produce any
herb

herb or vegetable whatever; where confequently not only men could never refide, but where no animal of any kind could poffibly exift. The journal itfelf confutes that opinion; in which the attentive reader will perceive that frequent mention is made of the ruins of buildings, which in all probability are only fmall remains of what once exifted on thofe fpots. Before the difcovery of the paffage round the Cape of Good Hope, when the productions of the Eaft were neceffarily brought part of the way to Europe by land, particularly in the remote ages of antiquity; the great defert was doubtlefs one of the principal channels of eaftern commerce. At that time I fuppofe thofe buildings to have been erected, nor can I attribute the exiftence of Palmyra itfelf, which is fituated in a moft barren part of the defert, to any other caufe. Water the great principal of both animal and vegetable life is not wanting. By means of thofe ravines or water courfes which communicate with the Euphrates, and alfo from the wells which are interfperfed throughout the defert; water enough might be obtained, not only for domeftic ufes, but alfo to anfwer the purpofes of hufbandry. The foil in general is by no means fo barren as not to be capable of cultivation; there are but few fpots that would not yield to the perfevering hand of induftry.

R r   Should

Should the Chriftian powers hereafter drive the
Turks out of Europe, and compel them to retreat
beyond the bounds of Afia Minor; it is by no means
improbable that towns and villages would then rife
up on what is now called the defert; and the remains of thofe barren fpots again become, what I
believe them to have formerly been, only intermediate commons; like Salifbury plain, or Bagfhot
heath. .

In defcribing the Arabs, a perfon ought to enter into very nice difcriminations, for every tribe
has its peculiar character; but as it is intended on
this occafion to vindicate them only from the common imputation of being faithlefs favages; I fhall
content myfelf for the prefent with giving a flight
fketch of the moft ftriking features of a defert A-
rab's mind. He like the reft of his fellow crea-
tures is much governed by felf-love; but this paffion is fo tempered and qualified in him, by the
liberal dictates of honour and hofpitality; and the
mild and benevolent influence of pity, and com-
paffion; as to preferve his uncultivated mind from
finking into abfolute felfifhnefs: thefe fentiments
and paffions correct even the violence of his religion's prejudices, and render him equally humane
to a conquered enemy, whether a Chriftian, or a
Mahomedan. Many circumftances mentioned in

the

the preceding journal prove that this is a faithful
outline of their character, and very different from
the idea generally entertained of these people. The
Bedouins who attacked us near Tiaba could certainly have cut us to pieces and made themselves
masters of the whole of our property, but they
preferred obtaining from us a moderate tribute for
the merchandize belonging to Khwaja Rubens, and
the Bagdad caravan. Their right to exact a tribute
from passengers may perhaps be disputed; but it
must be remembered that they are lords of the defert, and will be paid a duty for all merchandize
that passes through their territories. Some caravans it is true are powerful enough to resist, and
refuse to comply with their demands; and so do
the armies of Prussia, Austria, and France force
their way through the dominions of the smaller
states of Germany: but a Frenchman must pay
custom-house duties for his goods in Germany; as
must a German satisfy the demands of government
in France.

Our caravan was attacked a second time, but we
were too powerful for our adversaries, in consequence of which a treaty took place, and fourteen
of their people joined our party; nor during the
remainder of our journey did the least mark of ill-

humour

humour or refentment break out between our people and their new affociates. It is true, that the Arabs who plundered Mr. Borel acted apparently in the firft inftance towards him with unwarrantable violence; but I am convinced they would not have gone fuch lengths had they found him difpofed to treat and to pay them, as we did, a moderate tribute. In the engagement Mr. Borel killed feveral of their comrades; neverthelefs when he recovered and implored their mercy, no man could have fhewn more honour or fpirit than the old Sheick did in his defence, which could only have proceeded from the moft laudable and difinterefted motives; for it is evident from their fituation, that Mr. Borel had no opportunity of promifing him any reward for his protection. To thefe might be added many other inftances of equal honour and humanity fhewn by the Arabs to Europeans, collected even from the accounts of thofe who complain moft of ill treatment from them; but I flatter myfelf that thofe I have already mentioned, together with the remarkable inftances of liberality in the old Sheick when I fettled accounts with him; are fufficient teftimonies of their poffeffing fentiments and paffions that place them much above the rank of unfeeling barbarians.

THAT

THAT some unfortunate travellers may have suffered from their violence and rapacity, I do not dispute; there are thieves and affassins in all parts of the inhabited globe; and into whose hands strangers, not properly introduced, are most likely to fall: but in most of the accounts I have read complaining of the Arabs, I have found great reason to believe that the sufferings of the Europeans originated in their own imprudence, or else in the treachery of their Interpreters. The books of travels in Europe are filled with melancholy stories of hair-breadth escapes from robbery and murder, and constant lamentations of insults and impositions. Why then are we to villify the characters of all the Arabs, and represent them as destitute of principle, because a person unacquainted with their language, or their manners and customs, has experienced the same ill treatment from the worst of their countrymen, as he would have been liable to meet with in any country in Europe? With equal propriety might a foreigner accuse all English men of being cheats, and highwaymen; because one of his countrymen has been imposed on at an inn; or robbed on the road between Dover and London. To sum up all that need be said on this subject for the present in a few words. An European who wishes to pass the desert with ease and safety,

must

muſt lay aſide all his own prejudices, and not ridi-
cule thoſe of the Arabs. Before he ſets out he
ſhould have all their claims clearly aſcertained—
behave to them on the way with kindneſs without
familiarity—and in ſettling accounts at the end of
the journey, be liberally juſt to them, without
profuſion.

THE END.

SUPPLEMENT

CONTAINING

LISTS of the STAGES

IN THE

DIFFERENT ROUTS

FROM

ENGLAND to BASSORA,

TAKEN

Either from the JOURNALS and OBSERVATIONS

Of the AUTHOR,

OR

Collected by him from the BEST AUTHORITIES.

———————————————

IT has been obferved that a perfon going to *India* acrofs the great defert, had better embark at fome of the parts of *Italy* or *France*, and from thence proceed to *Aleppo*, either by *Latichea* or *Alexandretta*: but that a difpatch fhould be fent through *Vienna* and *Conftantinople*, directly to

2 *Bag-*

SUPPLEMENT.

Bagdad*; or elfe by *Aleppo*, to *Baffora*. Could I fuppofe this advice would invariably be followed, it would be unneceffary to take any further notice of the route by *Conftantinople*, which in this cafe would be frequented only by couriers: but as curiofity may induce travellers who can command their time, to pafs that way; I have collected with all poffible care, correct lifts of the different ftages through *France*, the *Netherlands*, and *Holland* to *Vienna*; and fo on by *Conftantinople*, to *Aleppo*, and from thence by various routes to *Baffora*.

---

* A merchant who long refided at *Conftantinople* and traded from thence to *Bagdad*, fays; that when at the former, he frequently received expreffes from the latter city in twelve or fourteen days. The diftance is eftimated at fix hundred and fifty Englifh miles. He is not acquainted with the name of each particular ftage; but he fays the couriers pafs through *Tokut* or *Tokaiah*, where there is a manufacture of porcelaine; and *Gemmifh Hanar*, near the filver mines, and fo by *Diarbekir* to *Bagdad*.

SUPPLEMENT.

POSTS from CALAIS through STRASBURG to VIENNA.

Names of Places	Posts	Names of Places	Posts
Calais		Brought over	56½
to		Toul	1½
Ardres	2	Velaine	1½
La Recousse	1	Nancy	1½
St. Omer	2	Domballe	1½
Aire	2	Luneville	1½
Lillers	1½	Benaminil	1½
Bethune	1½	Blamont	2
Souchet	2	Hening	2
Arras	1½	Saarburg	1
Herville	½	Himmartin	1
Bapaume	1	Phalgburg	1
{ Sailly en { Auronaise	1	Souerne	1½
Peronne	1½	Wiltheim	2
Beauvoir	2	Stiffein	1
St. Quentin	1½	Strasbourg	1½
Cerisy	1½		
La Fere	1½	French Posts	77
Laon	2½		
Corbeny	2½	Kehl	1
Berry au bac	1	Bishoffocira	1
Reims	2	Stolhuffen	1
Petites loges	2½	Radstatt	1
Chalons	2½	Erlinghen	1
Chepi	1	Durlach	1
La Chauffie	1	Pforzheim	1½
St. Amand	1	Entzwangen	1
Vitry Le Francais	1	Conftadt	1½
Longchamp	2½	Blockinhen	1½
St. Dizier	1½	Gofppinghen	1
Saaldrupt	1½	Geifslinghen	1
Bar le duc	1½	Westerfteiten	1
Ligny	2	Ulm	1
St. Aubin	1	Gunzburg	1½
Void	1½	Susmarshausen	1½
Layes	1½	Augsburg	1½
		Everfburg	1½
Carried over	56½	Carried over	21

POSTS from CALAIS, &c.

Names of Places	Poſts
Brought over	21
Schwalhauſen —	1½
MUNICH —	1½
Anzing —	1½
Haag —	1½
Humpfing —	1½
Alten Oeting —	1½
Mackel —	1½
Braunau —	1
Altheim —	1
Ried —	1½
Unterhaag —	1
Lambach —	1½
Vells —	1
LINTZ —	2
Ens —	1½
Screnberg —	1
Amſtatten —	1½
Kemmelbach —	1
Molk —	1½
St. Polten —	1½
Perſchling —	1
Sichartſkirchen —	1
Burkersdorf —	1
VIENNA —	1
German Poſts	53½

Note, The French Poſt on an average is five Engliſh miles. The German Poſt on an average is nearly twelve Engliſh miles.

POSTS from OSTENDE by COLOGNE to VIENNA.

Oſtende to	
BRUGES —	2
Alter —	2
GHENT —	2
Quadregt —	1
Aloſt —	1½
Carried over	8½

Names of Places	Poſts
Brought over	7
Aſche —	1½
BRUSSELS —	1½
Louvain —	3
Tirlemont —	2
St. Trond —	2
Tongern —	1½
MAESTRICHT —	1
AIX —	2
Juliers —	1½
Bergen —	1
COLOGNE —	1½
	27

Note, At *Cologne* the route from *Helvoetſluyt*, and that from *Oſtende* meet.

POSTS from HELVEOTSLUYS through FRANKFORT and RATISBON to VIENNA.

Helveotſluys to	Poſts	Hours
ROTTERDAM —		12½
Dort —		4½
Gorcum —		4
Loveſtein Caſtle —		½
Bommel, on the river Waal		3½
Nimeguen —	2	
CLEVES —	2	
Santen —	2	
Hockſtrat —	2	
Nuys —	1	
Dormain —	1	
COLOGNE —	1	
Bonn —	2	
Remagen —	1½	
Andernach —	1½	
Coblentz —	1	
Naſſau —	1½	
Naſteden —	1	
Carried over	19½	

SUPPLEMENT.

POSTS from *Helveotsluys*, &c.

Names of Places		Posts
Brought over		19½
* *Schwalbach*	—	1
MAYENCE	—	1½
Hadersheim	—	1
†FRANKFORT *on the* MAINE	—	1
HANAU	—	1½
Dettingen	—	1
Aschaffenburg	—	1
Besenbach	—	1¼
Rolwibrun	—	1
Eselbach	—	1
Romling	—	1
WURTZBURG	—	1
Kitzingen	—	1½
Possenheim	—	1½
Langenfeld	—	1
Emskirchen	—	1
Farabach	—	1¼
NURENBURGH	—	1
Teucht	—	1
Poschbaur	—	1
Teining	—	1
Tagwang	—	1
Hohen Schambach	—	1
§RATISBON	—	1
Pfader	—	1½
Straubingen	—	1½
Platling	—	2
Vilshofen	—	2
Passau	—	2
Eissenbein	—	1
Enzenkirchen	—	1
Carried over		57

* Or from *Schwalbach* to *Wisbaden* 1 post; to *Hadersheim* 1½; to *Frankfort* 1 post.

† In going during the summer season from *Frankfort* towards the *Netherlands* or *Holland*; it is very pleasant to pass by water to the place of destination.

§ It is also in summer a very pleasant voyage down the *Danube* from *Ratisbon* to *Vienna*.

Names of Places		Posts
Brought over		57
Beyerbach	—	1
Efferding	—	1½
Lintz	—	1½
Ens	—	1½
Stremberg	—	1
Amstatten	—	1½
Kemmelbach	—	1
Moelk	—	1½
St. Polten	—	1½
Perschling	—	1
Sichartskirchen	—	1
Burkersdorf	—	1
VIENNA	—	1
		72½

POSTS from FRANKFORT to AUGSBURG.

Frankfort to		
Hanau	—	1
Dettingen	—	1
Aschaffenbourg	—	1
Obenburgh	—	1
Miltenbourg	—	1
Hundheim	—	1
Bischoffsheim	—	1
Merganthein	—	1
Blaufelden	—	1½
Creilsheim	—	1½
Dinkespull	—	1
Oetinen	—	1½
Wending	—	1½
Donawert	—	1½
Meittengen	—	1½
AUGSBURG	—	1½
		19½

SUPPLEMENT.

ROUT from FRANCKFORT and AUGSBURG to INSPRUCK through TRENT to VENICE.		POSTS from VIENNA to CONSTANTINOPLE by the Way of BELGRADE.	
Names of Places	Posts	Names of Places	Posts
*AUGSBURG		Hochan	1
to Schwabmuchen	1½	Wimpussing	1
to Bucklor. —	1	G·js H ßein	1
to Kaufbeyren	1	Vendenburg	1
to Staten	1	Waraisdorff	1
to Fuessen —	1	Guntz	1
to Haydcrwang	1	Stein Am Anger	1
to Lermes —	1	Kormend	1½
to Nazareith —	1	Szala Egeszegh	2
to Payerwis —	1	Kahot	1½
to INSPRUCK —	1	Gross Kanisa	1½
to Schonberg —	1	Ibaros	1
to Stenach —	1	Bresnitz	1
to Breuner —	1	Babosca	1½
to Storzingen —	1	Isvaudi	1½
to Mittewald —	1	Gross Szigeth	1
to Brixen —	1	Saint Laurent	1
to Colman —	1	Funff Kirchen	1
to Teutschen —	1	Siklos	1½
to Bolzano —	1	Barangawar	1½
to Branzol —	1	Laskofeld	1
to Neumarkel —	1	Esseg	1
to St. Micheli —	1	Vera	1
to Trenta —	1	Vukovar	1
to Pergini —	1	Novosella	1
to Borgo —	2	Putsch	1½
to Primola —	2	Kereskitscha	1
to Bassano —	2	Gloschau	1
to Castel Franco	2½	Peterwardien	2
to Treviso —	1½	Carlowitz	1
to Maestri —	1½	Peska	1
to VENICE —	1½	Panosowa	2
		Semlin	2
	35½		41

Note, Semlin is 12 German miles from Vienna, and the last station in the German dominions going to Belgrade.

SUPPLEMENT.

POSTS from Vienna, &c.	Distance per Hours
From *Semlin* crofs the *Danube* to	
Belgrade —	¾
Krofka or *Ifaroik* —	5
Kolar —	4
Haffon Batha Palanka —	6
Batifchina —	7
Jagodina —	6
Mora va Hifar —.	4
Razna —	6
Alexintza —	4
Niffa, *on the river Niffowa*	6
Muftafa Pafha —	8
Sarquoi —	4
Saribrodi —	6
Sophia, *on the river Bagona*	6
Jegnikan —	5
Kliman —	7
Kifibifar —	6
Tzapar Bazageek —	6
Philipopoli, *on the river* *Marizza* —	6
Papuzli —	2¼
Quyali —	5¼
Ufum-tfiova —	3
Hermenli —	5
Muftafa Pafha —	4
Hebibchey —	3
Adrianople, *on the river* *Tungia Orta* and *Ma-rizza* —	7
Apla —	4
Efkibaba —	6
Burgufe —	4
Karefteran —	4
Schourli —	6
Kynicklu —	3½
Silibria —	4½
Ruyuk Chickmagee	6
Kutchuk Chickmagee	3
Constantinople	3
	176½

ROUT from Constantinople to Aleppo. Names of Places	Order of Posts	Distance by Hours
Constantinople acrofs the *Hellefpont* to *Scuder* or *Scutari* —	1	
Scuder or *Chryfopolis* to *Gheibize*	1	8
Between this poft & the next you ferry acrofs the Gulph of *Nicomedia* to *Herfek*	2	12½
Chiniflik —	3	6
Leuke —	4	10
Sckut —	5	7
Efki Shaher —	6	10
Saidee Kbazze —	7	9
Cofruff Batha —	8	13
Ballawadin —	9	6
Iffaklee —	10	7
Akfhehar —	11	10
Il Ghaun —	12	18
Conia —	13	21
Karabcenar —	14	10
Eraglie, olim *Heraclea*	15	12
Ururifla —	16	10
Adena —	17	16
Kat Callah —	18	12
Byafs —	19	9
Bylan —	20	7
Antioch by *Salkin*	21	10
Aleppo —	22	36
	Hrs.	260½

N. B. On account of the troubles in the road from *Adena* to *Antioch*; the thieves having driven the Turkifh governor from *Byafs* and eftablifhed themfelves in it; Mr. Baldwin was forced to take the other road, as in his journal, by *Caradafh*; but upon his return he had an efcort from the thieves, and took the road as above.

Note, An hour's travelling is eftimated at three Englifh miles.

SUPPLEMENT.

ABSTRACT of the foregoing JOURNAL.

Names of Places	Hours	Names of Places	Hours
ROUT from ALEPPO to BASSORA, directly across the great desert.		Brought over	125
		Haglet ul Havran —	10
			6
ALEPPO			9
to		*Ruined Village* —	9
Neyreb —	3		16
Haglier —	9	*Rabaly* —	3¼
Afbuck Mafbook	7¼		10
	11		10
	8	*Hidia* —	5
	9	*Birket Rabama* —	4¼
	8	*Alatbe*, two small forts	5
	7¼		9¼
	8		9¼
	9		8¼
Juab Kunnum, or *Ain-ul-Horoof*	8½		9¼
	8		9
	9½		9
	9¼		9
	9		10
		Cosbda —	3
		Zabeer —	3⅝
Carried over	125	BASSORA —	3½
		Total Hours	227¼

A JOURNEY over the little desert of ARABIA from ALEPPO to BAGDAD and SEMMEVA by the EUPHRATES to BASSORA.

Names of Places	Hours		Computed English miles	Remarks
To *Spheree* —	5	0	11⅞	Fine clear rivulets of water.
Remained encamped at *Spheree*.				
Hagla — —	4	12	9⅞	Well of bad water.
Has Meferr —	8	30	19⅞	No water.
Anda Veaugul —	9	15	20⅝	No water.
{ *Elga*, or { *Tchieltiore* —	10	30	23½	No water.

SUPPLEMENT.

JOURNEY, &c. by the *Euphrates* to BASSORA.

Names of Places	Hours		Computed English miles	Remarks
Near *Ain il Kom* or *Koum* —	7	30	16 7/8	Bad water.
At *Ain ul Koum* —	1	30	3 3/8	Good water.
The plain of *Geboul Bushier* —	8	30	19 4/8	No water.
Hopra Fadle —	10	0	22 4/8	No water.
Ferrasche —	6	30	14 5/8	Two wells of bad water.
Geboul Bushier —	8	45	19 1/8	No water.
Dickaynia —	8	0	18	Several wells of bad water.
The desert on the rout to *Routgaugh*	3	0	6 6/8	No water.
Routgaugh, or *Rutgar* —	8	0	18	No water.
Quoerlastep —	8	30	19 5/8	Little rain water in the rocks.
Gelta — —	9	15	20 6/8	No water.
Anna — —	9	0	20 2/8	Euphrates.
Passed from the northward of the town to the south —	1	30	3 3/8	Along the Banks of Euphrates.
Encamped.				
Remained encamped.				
Crossed the *Euphrates* to				Encamped along the Euphrates.
Der Mahomet —	5	0	11 2/8	
El Masace —	7	30	16 7/8	Ditto.
From *Masace* left the caravan and with 13 camels travelled expeditiously to				
Thir or *Thur* —	9	45	31 1/8	No water.
To the northward of *Bagdad* salt plain	9	20	30 2/8	No Water.
Desert from the salt plain in the night	6	0	19 4/8	Well water.
Over a level desert and the beaten track of the salt caravan	8	30	27 1/8	Passed two wells of tolerable water.

JOURNEY, &c. by the *Euphrates* to BASSORA.			
Names of Places	Hours	Computed English miles	Remarks
Same track in the night	3 10	11¾	Suppose there is water, but being night could not see
over {A very level desert and the beaten track of the salt caravans to *Bagdad* —	9 30	30⅞	Several wells and reservoirs of good water. River *Tigris*.

ROUTE from BAGDAD to SEMMEVA with mules or jack asses each carrying about one hundred and fifty pounds weight.

Names of Places				Miles	Hours
•BAGDAD to *Azad*	—	—	—	13	4 30
Berranst	—	—	—	6	2 0
Secundera	—	—	—	7½	2 30
Mabavil	—	—	—	12	4 0
Hillah	—	—	—	11	3 45
Emmam Ali	—	—	—	30	10 0
Ramahie, with horses loaded	—	20	6 0
Semmeva	—	—	—	52	16 0

	Miles
The distance from *Aleppo* to *Bagdad* —	466
Bagdad to *Semeva* —	151
Semmeva to *Bassora* by water	257

Total from *Aleppo* to *Bassora* 874

* From *Bagdad* there are two passages to *Bassora*, one by the *Tigris*, the other by the *Euphrates*: that by the former is described in the following extract from the journal of Capt. Elliot Elliots; of the latter many accounts have been already given.

"On the 15th of April we took a bark to pass down the *Tigris* from *Bagdad* to *Bassora*. This river below *Bagdad* has two arms, one of which runs along the side of the ancient *Chaldea*, and the other towards the point of *Mesopotamia*: and they both form a large island, which is traversed by several small canals. When we came to the place where the two arms part, we saw what we took to be ruins of an ancient town, near three miles in compass. The walls that remain are so large, that six coaches may pass along them abreast at the same time. They are made of bricks burnt in the fire, each of which was ten feet square and three thick. We took that branch of the *Tigris* which runs along the side of *Chaldea*, for fear of falling into the lands of the Arabs; who at that time were at war with the Bashaw of *Bagdad*. We were

; ten

SUPPLEMENT.

THE following voyage up the EUPHRATES from BASSORA to HILLA and the itinerary from thence to BAGDAD, MOSUL, and DIARBEKIR, to ALEPPO, is extracted from the voyage of Mr. Ives.

APRIL 27th, 8 o'clock in the morning embarked, and by means of a fair wind and the affistance of the tide went 75 miles. 28th, paffed *Corna* or *Querne*, a town fituated at the conflux of the two rivers *Tigris* and *Euphrates*. 29th, tracked to *Moufurat*, an Arab village. 30th, paffed feveral Arab villages, particularly *Moothalban*. May 1, paffed *Nawafhe* a town, and *Cota* an Arab village. Tracked 2d *Arijia*, an Arab village tracked with difficulty. 3d, tracked to *Grayhim* an Arab town; from hence the branch of a large river communicates with the *Tigris*. 4th, tracked; 5th, tracked; 6th, tracked to the town of *Semmeva*. 7th, tracked with difficulty. 8th, tracked near *Monzaradab.* 9th, tracked to the town of *Sembleeu.* 10th, tracked to *Dewana* in the government of *Hafeus* 11th, halted at *Dewana* to vifit the governor. 12, afternoon, tracked and paffed the fort of *Monoly*. 13th, pleafant country tracked. 14th, tracked; 15th, tracked. 16th, tracked, and paffed the village *Affia*, *Ijadea*, *Venahaara*, *Zada*, *Chili*, *Dulab*, and at two o'clock in the afternoon arrived at *Hilla**. As the *Euphrates* at this place turns to the N. W. tra-

ten days in paffing from *Bagdad* to *Baffora*, and lay every night in the bark, and there dreffed our victuals. When we came to any village we fent our people to purchafe provifions, which they bought very cheap. The names of the villages by the fide of this river are *Amurat*, where there is a fort conftructed of burnt bricks; *Sataral*, with a fint of the fame kind; *Manfury*, a large town; *Mazar*, *Gazar*, and *Corna*. This laft place ftands on the point at the confluence of the *Euphrates*, and *Tigris*. It has three fmall caftles, or forts, one of which ftands upon the point, and is the ftrongeft of the three; the fecond is on the fide of *Chaldea*; and the third on that of *Arabia*. The maps call this cit. *Kurna* under which denomination it is beft known."

* You may poffibly reach *Hilla* on the *Euphrates* from *Baffora* in 12 days, but they are commonly 15 or 20 in their paffage thither. From thence you may travel over the land to *Bagdad* in two days, and the journeys are but fhort neither. If you go up the *Tigris* you will be all the time upon the water; I would therefore advife you, as well on that account as for the fake f expedition, to take horfes at *Ijmark.* When you are arrived at *Bagdad*, you are again to confider whether you will travel by the way of *Kubeffa*, and over the little defert by *Meful*, which lies farther up the *Tigris*. The time fpent in paffing over the little defert is fourteen or fifteen days, and you muft make the fame kind of provifion as for travelling over the great defert. I muft confefs, I think this road deferves the preference. Europeans have frequently travelled this way fingly. Having croffed the *Tigris* you muft travel by land till you come to *Anna*, where you pafs the *Euphrates*; but it will be neceffary to procure a pafs, which will be no difficult matter to obtain, if you have a proper recommendation from *Baffora*.

b 2

W. travellers muſt go by land to *Bagdad*, which ſtands on the *Ti-gris* at the diſtance of about 50 miles from *Hilla* N. W.

May 17th accompanied by a ſmall caravan and five Turk-iſh horſemen at five P. M. left *Hilla*, and in five hours arrived at *Mahoul Kauri*. 18th, *Serai* at *Eſcanderab* 15 miles, which being dirty proceeded to *Horta*, about eight miles further. 19th, march about 9 miles to *Azaup Serai*, a little beyond which the city of *Bagdad* is ſeen.

			Miles
From *Baſſora* to *Corna*	—	—	75
to *Cota*	—	—	69
to *Semmeva*	—	—	147
to *Lembleon*	—	—	65
to *Aſſia*	—	—	31
to *Hilla*	—	—	52
to *Bagdad*	—	—	50
			489

JOURNEY from BAGDAD to ALEPPO as performed by Mr. Ives and his party.

June 19th.

					Hours
Left *Bagdad* ſeven in the evening, and arrived at *Yankjab* in				—	7
and from thence proceeded to *Dakehalab*				—	1
Kann Muſabab	—	—	—	—	6
Chiba Harpſie river	—	—	—	—	4
Dely abas couprie Kaun	—	—	—	—	4
Kaſcada-wirt, mountains	—	—	—	—	2
Narin, river	—	—	—	—	3
Karatapa	—	—	—	—	5
Aſke couprie	—	—	—	—	$7\frac{1}{2}$
The *Courmaratida* mountains in ſight to the right.					
Danzcourmatu	—	—	—	—	$8\frac{1}{2}$
Tawook	—	—	—	—	$7\frac{1}{4}$
Gergoot	—	—	—	—	9
Alton couprie	—	—	—	—	9
Yengee Kaun	—	—	—	—	6
Arvele	—	—	—	—	$4\frac{1}{2}$
Zarp, river	—	—	—	—	$8\frac{1}{2}$
Zaave	—	—	—	—	1
Camaliſk Gawerkoe	—	—	—	—	5
Ninroeb, a ſmall village, reputed to be the ruins of ancient					
Ninroeb	—	—	—	—	$5\frac{1}{2}$
				Mofül	

Journey, &c. by the *Euphrates* to Bassora.			
Names of Places	Hours	Computed English miles	Remarks
Same track in the night	3 10	11¾	Suppofe there is water, but being night could not fee
over A very level defert and the beaten track of the falt caravans to *Bagdad* —	9 30	30¾	Several wells and refervoirs of good water. River *Tigris*.

ROUTE from BAGDAD to SEMMEVA with mules or jack affes each carrying about one hundred and fifty pounds weight.

Names of Places		Miles	Hours	
*BAGDAD to *Azad*	— — —	13	4	30
Berranzft	— — —	6	2	0
Secundera	— — —	7½	2	30
Mabavil	— — —	12	4	0
Hillab	— — —	11	3	45
Emmam Ali	— — —	30	10	0
Ramabie, with horfes loaded —		20	6	0
Semmeva	— — —	52	16	0

		Miles
The diftance from *Aleppo* to *Bagdad*	—	466
Bagdad to *Semiva*		151
Semmeva to *Baffora* by water		257

Total from *Aleppo* to *Baffora* 874

* From *Bagdad* there are two paffages to *Baffora*, one by the *Tigris*, the other by the *Euphrates*: that by the former is defcribed in the following extract from the journal of Capt. Elliot Elliots; of the latter many accounts have been already given.
"On the 15th of April we took a bark to pafs down the *Tigris* from *Bagdad* to *Baffora*. This river below *Bagdad* has two arms, one of which runs along the fide of the ancient *Chaldea*, and the other towards the point of *Mefopotamia*: and they both form a large ifland, which is traverfed by feveral fmall canals. When we came to the place where the two arms part, we faw what we took to be ruins of an ancient town, near three miles in compafs. The walls that remain are fo large, that fix coaches may pafs along them abreaft at the fame time. They are made of bricks burnt in the fire, each of which was ten feet fquare and three thick. We took that branch of the *Tigris* which runs along the fide of *Chaldea*, for fear of falling into the hands of the Arabs; who at that time were at war with the Bafhaw of *Bagdad*. We were

; ten

SUPPLEMENT.

The following voyage up the EUPHRATES
from BASSORA to HILLA and the itinerary from thence to BAGDAD, MOSUL,
and DIARBEKIR, to ALEPPO, is extracted
from the voyage of Mr. IVES.

APRIL 27th, 8 o'clock in the morning
embarked, and by means of a fair wind and the assistance of the
tide went 75 miles. 28th, passed *Corna* or *Querne*, a town situated
at the conflux of the two rivers *Tigris* and *Euphrates*. 29th, tracked to *Moufurat*, an Arab village. 30th, passed several Arab villages, particularly *Moochalban*. May 1, passed *Nacwasse* a town,
and *Cota* an Arab village. Tracked 2d *Arijia*, an Arab village
tracked with difficulty. 3d, tracked to *Graybim* an Arab town;
from hence the branch of a large river communicates with the *Tigris*. 4th, tracked; 5th, tracked; 6th, tracked to the town of
Semmeva. 7th, tracked with difficulty. 8th, tracked near *Mon-
zuradab*. 9th, tracked to the town of *SemLieu*. 10th, tracked to
Dewana in the government of *Hafeu* 11th, halted at *Dewana* to
visit the governor. 12, afternoon, tracked and passed the fort of
Monoly. 13th, pleasant country tracked. 14th, tracked; 15th,
tracked. 16th, tracked, and passed the village *Affia, Ifjadea, Venahaara, Zada, Chili, Dulab*, and at two o'clock in the afternoon
arrived at *Hilla*[*]. As the *Euphrates* at this place turns to the N.
W. tra-

---

ten days in passing from *Bagdad* to *Bassora*, and lay every night in the bark, and there
dressed our victuals. When we came to any village we sent our people to purchase
provisions, which they bought very cheap. The names of the villages by the side of
this river are *Amurat*, where there is a fort constructed of burnt bricks; *Satarat*, with
a fort of the same kind; *Manfury*, a large town; *Muxar, Gazar*, and *Corna*. This
last place stands on the point at the confluence of the *Euphrates*, and *Tigris*. It has
three small castles, or forts, one of which stands upon the point, and is the strongest
of the three; the second is on the side of *Chaldea*; and the third on that of *Arabia*.
The maps call this cit. *Kurna* under which denomination it is best known."

[*] You may possibly reach *Hilla* on the *Euphrates* from *Bassora* in 12 days, but they are
commonly 15 or 20 in their passage thither. From thence you may travel over
the land to *Bagdad* in two days, and the journeys are but short neither. If you go
up the *Tigris* you will be all the time upon the water; I would therefore advise you,
as well on that account as for the sake of expedition, to take horses at *Ijmark*. When
you are arrived at *Bagdad*, you are again to consider whether you will travel by the
way of *Kubessa*, and over the little desert by *Mesul*, which lies farther up the *Tigris*.
The time spent in passing over the little desert is fourteen or fifteen days, and you
must make the same kind of provision as for travelling over the great desert. I
must confess, I think this road deserves the preference. Europeans have frequently
travelled this way singly. Having crossed the *Tigris* you must travel by land till you
come to *Anna*, where you pass the *Euphrates*; but it will be necessary to procure a
pass, which will be no difficult matter to obtain, if you have a proper recommendation from *Bassora*.   b 2

SUPPLEMENT.

W. travellers muſt go by land to *Bagdad*, which ſtands on the *Tigris* at the diſtance of about 50 miles from *Hilla* N. W.

May 17th accompanied by a ſmall caravan and five Turkiſh horſemen at five P. M. left *Hilla*, and in five hours arrived at *Mahoul Kauri*. 18th, *Serai* at *Eſcanderab* 15 miles, which being dirty proceeded to *Horta*, about eight miles further. 19th, march about 9 miles to *Axaup Serai*, a little beyond which the city of *Bagdad* is ſeen.

				Miles
From *Baſſora* to *Corna*	—	—		75
to *Cota*	—	—		69
to *Semmeva*	—	—		147
to *Lembloon*	—	—		65
to *Aſſea*	—	—		31
to *Hilla*	—	—		52
to *Bagdad*	—			50
				489

JOURNEY from BAGDAD to ALEPPO as performed by Mr. Ives and his party.

June 19th.

					Hours
Left *Bagdad* ſeven in the evening, and arrived at *Yankjab* in					7
and from thence proceeded to *Dakebalab*				—	1
Kann Muſabab	—	—	—	—	6
Chiba Harpſee river	—	—	—	—	4
Dely abas couprie Kaun	—	—	—	—	4
Kuſcadawire, mountains	—	—	—	—	2
Narin, river	—	—	—	—	3
Karatapa	—	—	—	—	5
Aſke couprie	—	—	—	—	7½
The *Courmaratida* mountains in ſight to the right.					
Danzcourmatu	—	—	—	—	8½
Tawook	—	—	—	—	7¼
Gergoot	—	—	—	—	9
Alton couprie	—	—	—.	—	9
Yergec Kaun	—	—	—	—	6
Arvela	—	—	—	—	4¼
Zarp, river	—	—	—	—	8½
Zaavi	—	—	—	—	1
Camaliſk Gawerkot	—	—	—	—	5
Nineveh, a ſmall village, reputed to be the ruins of ancient *Nineveh*				—	5¼
				Moſul	

SUPPLEMENT.

A TABLE of the Diftance between each of the capital Cities and Towns in the Route from BASSORA to LATICHEA.

			Miles
From *Baffora* as before to *Bagdad*	——	489
Bagdad —— to *Gergoot*	——	167
Gergoot —— to *Arveta*	——	54
Arveta —— to *Moful*	——	49
Moful —— to *Nifibin*	——	103
Nifibin —— to *Arin*	——	26
Arin —— to *Diarbekir*	——	58
Diarbekir — to *Bir*	——	147
Bir —— to *Aleppo*	——	94
Aleppo —— to *Latichea*	——	102

Total of Miles 1289

FINIS.

SUPPLEMENT.

						Hours
†*Mosul*	—	—	—	—	—	6
Stayed six days at *Mosul.*						
Baduit, river	—	—	—	—	—	3½
Esche Mosul	—	—	—	—	—	5
					Tal.	

† " The caravans which pass by *Mosul*, which is the road we took, make a shorter cut over the Desert of *Tagut*, to the westward of the *Tigris*. We had the Bashaw of Bagdad's pass, which we found of very great service, for it procured us a very extraordinary respect wherever we came. Besides it exempted us from the visits of the custom-house people. Those who have no pass, had best gratify the custom-house officers with four or five Mamoudies, to prevent the opening of their baggage, though they have no right to demand any thing. The Turks are such lovers of money, that there is no danger in attempting to corrupt them in their office, for you may make your bargain in as plain terms as you please.

From *Bagdad* you may get to *Thourkat* or *Karkut* in eight days, and from thence to *Mosul* in four. If your stomach is a little nice, you had best provide yourself with eatables at *Bagdad*, for the bread and rice that you may meet with on the road may not possibly be white. However, the best bread is to be had at *Bassora*; and as for butter, you will meet with none after you leave that place till you come to *Aleppo*. As for our parts, we found the bread upon the road pretty good. As you travel along, you will meet with villages on the road to lodge in from stage to stage. But for the apartments they will be of little use, except to defend you from the weather; for there is no furniture, and it will be a rarity to find so much as a little stool. As for other conveniences, you are not to expect them. However, you may probably travel all along this road, as we did, by ourselves, without the least interruption or incivility.

At *Karkut*, which is a strong city, it is usual to rest a day or two and replenish your panniers; that is you must lay in provisions for four days at least, which is the time you will spend in going to *Mosul*, as mentioned above. As for wine, you must take care to supply yourself at *Bassora*, and that for a month or more. At *Bagdad* you may probably replenish your store as well as at *Karkut*; and at *Mosul* you must purchase provisions of all kinds for six days; as also at *Cojemser* or *Mardin* for *Orfar*, that is for six or eight days; and afterwards at that place for *Aleppo*, which is five days more; and among the Christians you will always meet with wine or brandy.

The place where you are most likely to be detained is *Mosul*, because you must either wait for a caravan, or hire a convoy; which last you may do at four rupees a man. If you will listen to them they will tell you, that it will be unsafe to travel without twenty or thirty of these people for a guard; but I am persuaded there is no such danger of robbers as they pretend. However there are caravans which set out from this place once in every ten or fourteen days, unless in the depth of winter, and they take a convoy, the money to pay which is levied by the Caravan Bashi, upon all the people of the caravan, generally in proportion to the goods which each person carries with him, but sometimes according to the number of beasts, and your share will consequently be but a trifle.

The usual time of travelling from *Mosul* to *Madan* or *Mardin* is eight days, and from *Mardin* to *Orfa* seven days. The first six days of the journey is over a desert almost without inhabitants, and therefore your fare will be good or bad according to the quality of the provisions you brought with you. Three days after you leave the *Tigris* the water begins to be brackish, and therefore it behoves you to take care to supply yourself with that which is good in time.

The caravan makes a halt at *Nisibin*, the next town to *Mosul*, where it is visited by the custom-house officers. But a gentleman that travels only with his baggage is

under

						Hours
Talmaſs, hill: the Sanjalk mountain on the left	—				—	5
Sefaga	—	—	—	—	—	8
Demir Rapee (a ſtream)		—	—	—	—	10
Geraza	—	—	—	—	—	6¼
Niſibin	—	—	—	—	—	7½
(From hence diſpatched a letter to the Conſul at *Aleppo*, to be delivered in ſeven days).						
Serka Kauu (a river)	—	—	—	—	—	1½
Aria	—	—	—	—	—	8
Mardin	—	—	—	—	—	2
Arrived at *Diarbekir* 21ſt July, two o'Clock afternoon, where we ſtayed	—	—	—	—	—	25
Inupu	—	—	—	—	—	24
Meniſſerab	—	—	—	—	—	12¼
N. B. *Urfa* the capital of a Baſhaw five hours S. W.						
From *Meniſſerab* to *Peſillekew* a valley, and the neighbouring village *Hauwah*	—	—	—	—	—	3
Cortocour, near a ſtream		—	—	—	—	12
Bir, or *Birjoup*, on the eaſtern banks of the *Euphrates*, a large town	—	—	—	—	—	5
Mazar (paſſed this village)		—	—	—	—	3
Encamped in a valley	—	—	—	—	—	1½
(From whence we diſpatched another letter to *Aleppo*, to be delivered in 24 hours).						
Saguera (a town and river)		—	—	—	—	4½
(Here we received a letter from the Conſul, at *Aleppo*).						
Caravanſarab		—	—	—	—	8
(From whence we abruptly left the Baſhaw and proceeded to *Aleppo*).						

under no necaſſity of ſtopping on that account, for he may proceed directly for *Cojumiſſer*, or *Cojafar*, which is a day's journey and a half farther. *Mardis* is a large town, about four or five miles out of the road, but it is worth ſeeing; and, which is a greater inducement, there is good wine to be had there, to ſerve you on the road to *Orfa*, which is five or ſix days journey more; and there likewiſe you will meet with people to make up a ſufficient caravan for the ſame road."

Vide Journal of Capt. Elliot Elliot.

A TABLE

SUPPLEMENT.

A TABLE of the Diftance between each of the capital Cities and Towns in the Route from BASSORA to LATICHEA.

				Miles
From *Baffora* as before to *Bagdad*			——	489
Bagdad	——	to *Gergoot*	——	167
Gergoot	——	to *Arbeta*	——	54
Arbeta	——	to *Moful*	——	49
Moful	——	to *Nifibin*	——	103
Nifibin	——	to *Arin*	——	26
Arin	——	to *Diarbekir*	——	58
Diarbekir	——	to *Bir*	——	147
Bir	——	to *Aleppo*	——	94
Aleppo	——	to *Latichea*	——	102

Total of Miles 1289

F I N I S.

acc: 13803

Observations on the Passage to India Through Egypt

yea: 1785